Endorsements

With wisdom and a sense of humor, Sha⸻ founding Book of Hosea to life. She skill⸻ historic facts, and thoughtful questions to show us how this book of the Bible still speaks and calls each one of us to "live loved." For those who want to go deeper, *God's Relentless Love* also contains a study guide.

Afton Rorvik, author of *Storm Sisters: Friends through All Seasons*

Sharla shows how Hosea's story mirrors God's relationship with the Israelites and then helps me humbly see myself in Gomer. I especially loved the section called "Live Like You're Loved"; it's a very down-to-earth, Gospel-centered approach to receiving God's love. The suggestions for group projects were a nice surprise—hands-on learning and application that many will enjoy. I encourage women to work through this Bible study together in small groups to become more acquainted with the Book of Hosea and to explore their own relationships with God.

Stephenie Hovland, author and educator

God's Relentless Love is a beautiful study of the Book of Hosea. Sharla guides the reader through this complicated book of the Bible and makes it relatable and understandable. As we learn about the Israelites and how they did not always trust God, we can see ourselves within the story. Instead of condemnation, God wraps us in His grace. He gently calls us back to the truth; He loves us unconditionally. God loves us, even when our faith is weak and when we forget about His faithfulness. We can rest in the promise that we are God's beloved children.

Michelle Diercks, podcast host of *Peace in His Presence*

The story of Hosea paints a stunning portrait of how God pursues the drifter and redeems the broken. Throughout this superb study, Sharla skillfully reminds us how God never fails to extend His loving grace every time we go spiritually AWOL. Through journaling, Scripture memorization, and honest insights, each chapter offers a fresh journey along antiquity's roads to demonstrate that we cannot outrun God or His affections. Sharla's study offered me much-needed space to dig deep into Scripture to discover once again that no matter how far I fall or how bad I mess up, God welcomes wanderers with His relentless love.

Donna Snow, author of *Forgiveness, Esther, Without This Ring,* and others; owner of Artesian Ministries

Beautiful, compelling, and full of wisdom. *God's Relentless Love*, a new Bible study by Sharla Fritz, helped me to better understand the dramatic love story of Hosea and Gomer. But more importantly, it helped me to understand God's unbelievable, totally gracious, infinite, tenacious, and all-knowing love for me. Sharla's well-researched study is filled with biblical wisdom, a deep dive into God's love for His people, and real-life stories of relentless love. It will forever change the way you understand Hosea—and will help you see how much you are loved by your heavenly Father.

Christina Hergenrader, author of *Family Trees and Olive Branches, Shine, Love Rules*, and others; retreat leader and speaker

Prepare yourself for a gripping love story—a true tale of a prophet and a prostitute, an ancient account as applicable today as it was then, unpacked in a most wonderful way. Author Sharla Fritz has woven history and prophecy together with engaging explanation, detailed context, and contemporary true tales, creating a Bible study masterpiece about *God's Relentless Love.* The story of Hosea's unwavering love for his unfaithful wife is also the story of God's relentless love for His rebellious people—His redeeming, restoring love for you and me in Christ. The message of this masterpiece is for anyone who has run after love, identity, or purpose apart from God, searching elsewhere in vain. *God's Relentless Love* enabled me to recognize modern ideas of idolatry that I've tried on for size, the worldly ways and means I've turned to instead of God, and the times I've doubted His love or drifted in a destructive direction. Above all, it allowed me to see with greater clarity God's unending pursuit, unlimited love, and unmatched mercy in Christ, my Savior!

Deb Burma, author of *Joy: A Study of Philippians*; *Living a Chocolate Life*; *Sip, Savor, and Drink Deeply*; and others; retreat leader and Christian speaker

GOD'S RELENTLESS LOVE

A STUDY OF HOSEA

SHARLA FRITZ

CONCORDIA PUBLISHING HOUSE · SAINT LOUIS

GOD'S
RELENTLESS
LOVE

Published by Concordia Publishing House
3558 S. Jefferson Ave., St. Louis, MO 63118-3968
1-800-325-3040 • cph.org

DEDICATION

To Steven and Shelly, who understand what it's
like to grow up in the center of the universe.

I so appreciate your talents in making me laugh!

Thanks for letting me share your
beautiful stories in this book.

Contents

Chapter Seven

Chapter Eight

INTRODUCTION

Do you enjoy a good love story? Do you race through novels with classic girl-meets-guy plots? Do you laugh and cry through rom-coms at the movie theater?

Personally, I love a funny, sweet, romantic tale that takes my mind off my own life's story, which usually contains either too many tangled twists or too much mundane monotony. However, romance novels disappoint me when I figure out how the story ends after reading only a few pages. I don't like a predictable plot.

No one would describe the Book of Hosea in the Old Testament as predictable. The Bible contains many love stories, but the account of

Timeline of the History of Israel

Rehoboam (931–914) Abijam (914–911)	Asa (911–870) Jehoshaphat (873–848)	Jehoram (853–841) Queen Athaliah (841–835) Joash (835–796)	Amaziah (796–767) Uzziah (790–7◄

950	900	850	800

950	900	850	800

Jeroboam (931–910) Nadab (910–909) Baasha (909–887)	Elah (886–885) Zimri (885) Tibni (885–880) Omri (885–874) Ahab (874–853)	Jehoram (852–841) Jehu (841–814) Jehoahaz (814–798)	Jehoash (798–78 Jeroboam II (793–753) Zedhariah (753–752)

the prophet Hosea and his unfaithful wife, Gomer, wins the prize for the most surprising. From the very beginning, where God Almighty directs His faithful messenger Hosea to marry a prostitute, to the ending that leaves us hanging, every chapter breaks the mold of a traditional tale of the heart.

If you've ever read the Book of Hosea, you may have scratched your head and wondered what it all meant. The book is confusing, cryptic, and complicated. Even if you make it through the strange love story, you encounter chapters of dire doom-and-gloom messages that Hosea delivered to the people of Israel.

So why bother with this complex and confounding account of a prophet and a prostitute? For a long time, I wondered that too. When I reached the Book of Hosea in my read-through-the-Bible-in-a-year plan, I usually

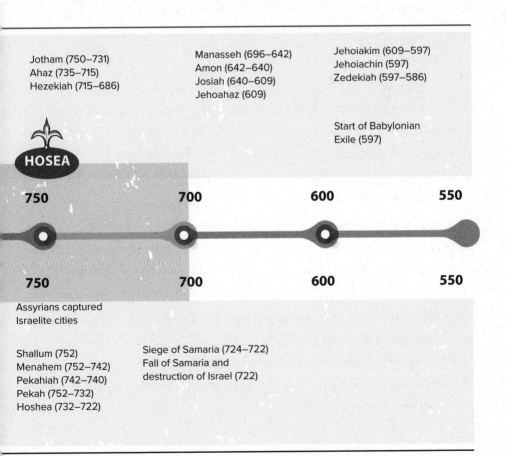

Jotham (750–731)
Ahaz (735–715)
Hezekiah (715–686)

Manasseh (696–642)
Amon (642–640)
Josiah (640–609)
Jehoahaz (609)

Jehoiakim (609–597)
Jehoiachin (597)
Zedekiah (597–586)

Start of Babylonian
Exile (597)

HOSEA

750   700   600   550

750   700   600   550

Assyrians captured
Israelite cities

Shallum (752)
Menahem (752–742)
Pekahiah (742–740)
Pekah (752–732)
Hoshea (732–722)

Siege of Samaria (724–722)
Fall of Samaria and
destruction of Israel (722)

skimmed the pages. I rushed through perplexing parts, not bothering to think about the imagery, not making the effort to find meaning for my life.

But one year, when I again finished the Book of Daniel and flipped the page to Hosea, the prophet's message came alive. I saw the unusual love story for what it was—a picture of God's relentless love for me. I saw that God cared for broken, sinful people like Gomer, like me. I rejoiced in the fact that I didn't need to have a pristine life before God could reach out to me. I cried tears of joy that I didn't have to make myself look good before God chose me and made me His own.

I won't give away the whole plot, but in this story of a prophet and his unfaithful wife, I saw the tale of my own life of faith. I understood more clearly that God constantly works to free me from my shackles of idolatry and entices me to leave my false gods. He desires an intimate relationship with me. He tells me I belong to Him and invites me to call Him "Husband."

Astounding.

To help you grasp the message of this book, we will examine it from a historical perspective, looking at what was happening in Israel at the time of Hosea. We'll look at the condition of the nation of Israel during this period and the symbolism of Hosea and Gomer's relationship. We'll study what Hosea's message meant to his original audience—Yahweh's chosen people.

God continues to speak through Hosea's words—their significance did not end with the Old Testament period. We'll look at how the Book of Hosea speaks to us as New Testament people. We'll apply the lessons of history to our own slice of time and our personal relationships with God.

Each chapter of this study begins with a contemporary story of relentless love. Family and friends have allowed me to share their inspiring tales of love that continue through difficulty, rejection, and time. I hope these narratives give you new perspectives of the story of God's relentless love for His people.

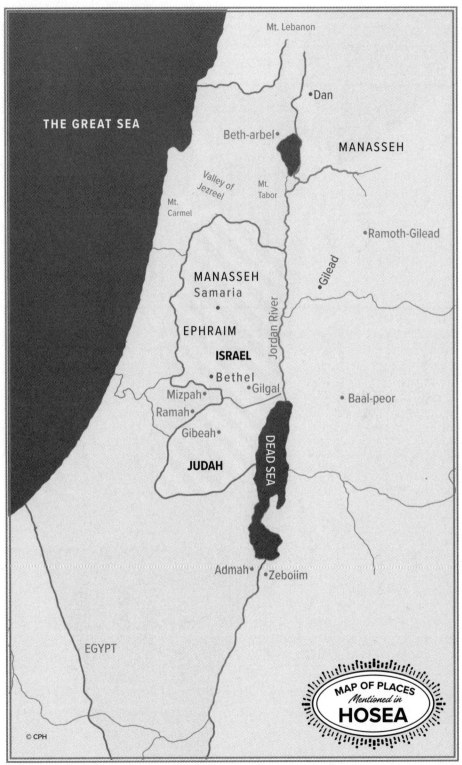

THE GREAT SEA

Mt. Lebanon

•Dan

Beth-arbel•

MANASSEH

Valley of Jezreel

Mt. Tabor

Mt. Carmel

•Ramoth-Gilead

•Gilead

MANASSEH
Samaria
•

Jordan River

EPHRAIM

ISRAEL

•Bethel
•Gilgal

Mizpah•
Ramah•

•Baal-peor

Gibeah•

DEAD SEA

JUDAH

Admah• •Zeboiim

EGYPT

MAP OF PLACES
Mentioned in
HOSEA

© CPH

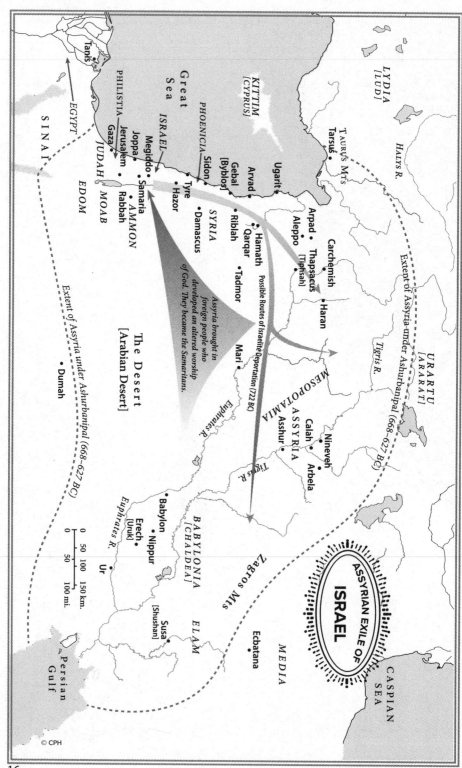

At the end of each chapter, I encourage you to "live like you're loved." I pray that Hosea and Gomer's unusual story helps the truth of God's unfailing love penetrate your soul. May the prophet's reassurance of the Lord's forgiveness drown out the voices of shame. May Hosea's message of God's passion for you overpower any heart-cries of doubt.

Why study Hosea? Because God saw fit to include it in His Holy Word, and therefore, He must have some significant message in it for us. Because it will help us abandon our modern, counterfeit gods. Because Hosea's ancient words will remind us that the Lord constantly pursues our hearts and works to restore our relationship with Him. Because this book invites us to live in God's relentless love.

USING THIS BOOK

Each chapter of *God's Relentless Love* explores one section of the Book of Hosea. By the time you have finished this study, you will have read the whole book and focused on its key concepts. As we trek through Hosea, the prophet will challenge us to examine the idols we may have and the worldly sources we turn to for help. However, Hosea will also remind us that God calls us by name and invites us to a life of intimacy with Him.

You may choose to study Hosea by reading straight through this book. The chapters include the following:

- Memory verses
- Contemporary stories of relentless love
- Historical information about life during Hosea's time
- What Hosea's message meant to his contemporaries
- What Hosea's message means to us as New Testament believers

In addition, I hope you will also take time to go deeper into the Book of Hosea by engaging in the study guide beginning on page 152. This section includes a variety of activities:

- Reflect on the Reading

- Dig into the Word

- Apply the Word to Your Life

- Create a Project

I encourage you to gather a few others to join you on this journey through Hosea. The study is designed to be completed in eight weeks, but if your meeting time is short or you simply want to take the journey a little more slowly, you may choose to devote two weeks to every chapter. You could complete the reading and the "Reflect on the Reading" questions one week, for example, and the "Dig into the Word," "Apply the Word to Your Life," and "Create a Project" sections the next week.

The "Create a Project" activities may be especially enjoyable to complete as a group. In fact, you might want to set out the materials for the activity so participants can work on it as they arrive for the study. You could also have the suggested songs playing in the background—tuning the hearts of everyone gathered to God's unfailing love.

Consider the following as you study:

- Begin with prayer.

- Rely on Scripture to guide your discussions.

- Keep what is shared confidential unless given permission to share outside the group.

May the Lord bless you as you immerse yourself in God's relentless love.

CHAPTER ONE

A Relentless Love Story

I stared at the name signed in blue crayon.

Who would send a letter that began, "Greetings and salutations (and, of course, felicitations for your academic achievements)"? Who would write cryptic questions like "What do you want out of life? What is the difference between a duck?"

From one of the lines in the puzzling letter, "I noticed your dossier in a recent publication," I knew that its author had seen my name in the *Wausau Daily Herald*. I had just graduated from high school with honors, and in my relatively small city of Wausau, Wisconsin, this meant getting my picture in the newspaper along with a list of achievements and the names of my parents.

In today's world where privacy is protected, getting such a letter would immediately set off alarms in anyone's brain. But back in the day when everyone was listed in the local phone book, we didn't worry much about stalking. Sure, this guy sounded a little odd, and it was unusual to receive a letter from someone I didn't know, but he made me laugh when he wrote, "I recently moved to the Wausau area. I am a graduate of Menomonee Falls East High and through a little hopskipping, and a bit of jumping, I have achieved junior status at the University of Wisconsin-Green Bay. I was going to say that I have a 3.91 overall GPA and 55 credits, which is fairly decent for one year's work, but I have decided that it would sound too pompous, so I won't tell you that."

Plus, he was an English major. At the time, I was plowing through a precollege reading list and was very frustrated with Shakespeare. Perhaps, at the least, this eccentric guy could help me decipher *The Tempest*. So I took a chance and wrote him back.

A few days later, he telephoned. We chatted for a while, and the mysterious young man—John—asked if I'd like to go out. I hesitated for a moment, but I said yes. (Growing up in a small city also made me very naive and trusting.)

We decided on a movie and pizza. Although the film I picked was possibly the worst movie I have ever seen, our conversation at Pizza Hut went much better.

So when John asked me out again, I said yes.

We spent a lot of time together that summer. He picked me up in his maroon Dodge Polara (a huge tuna boat of a car), and we would drive to the movie theater to watch a new flick or to a local park for a picnic. Or he would show up on his motorcycle, and we'd hang out at my house. It was a fun summer romance with a cute guy. At least, that was how I saw it. In the fall, I would begin touring with a Christian singing group, performing at churches and community centers around the country, and he would be focused on college. I didn't see how a long-term relationship could survive that scenario—even if I did enjoy being with him.

However, John saw things differently. He started talking about long-term plans for us—he was "getting serious." I was not ready for serious. Only eighteen, and in my first real boyfriend-girlfriend relationship, I simply wanted fun. So I broke off the relationship.

We did not keep in touch during that year on the road. But after I returned from my musical wanderings, John surprised me by calling me—to ask me for the phone numbers of some of my friends.

During that year of touring, I had learned a lot. About music. About life. About living with sixteen other people on a bus. And because of relationships that both formed and dissolved on that bus, I now realized what I had given up when I had given up on John.

So, instead of giving him my friends' phone numbers, I nervously asked if we could try again. I didn't know if he would overlook my previous rejection and give me another chance, but I did know I had to relinquish some pride to attempt a reconciliation.

Thankfully, John forgave all my past foolishness and we began again. We still had a long-distance relationship since we attended universities on opposite sides of Wisconsin. But we nurtured the relationship with letters, phone calls, and monthly visits.

Three years after receiving that cryptic letter, I married the guy who signed his name in blue crayon.

God's Relentless Love Calls You His Own

Hosea 1:1–2:1

MEMORY VERSE

Say to your brothers, "You are My people,"
and to your sisters, "You have received mercy."

Hosea 2:1

Rejection and reconciliation. Although Hosea's wife and I had very different backgrounds, the love story between the prophet and Gomer mirrors my own romantic tale. Hosea chronicles an account of love and loss and love again. His book tells the story of the relentless love of Hosea for his wife and of Yahweh for His chosen people. And for us as New Testament believers, it pictures the never-failing love of Christ for us—His Bride.

Just as my now-husband, John, gave our relationship a second chance, we will learn that Hosea took his wife back after she had left him. Just as my once-boyfriend called me after our breakup, God called out to the people of Israel after a long period of rebellion. Just as John forgave my rejection of him, God continually loves us and seeks to restore our relationship with Him after we have turned away and sought excitement in other places.

The Backstory

To better understand this Old Testament love story, we need to review a little history.

God's love story with Israel began when He promised Abraham that his family would become a great nation and occupy the land of Canaan (see Genesis 12:3–7; 17:4–8). Because of Abraham's faith and obedience, God blessed his descendants.

Why did Abraham's descendants become Yahweh's chosen nation? Later in Scripture, Moses gave the Israelites this message from the Lord:

> For you are a people holy to the LORD your God. The LORD your God has chosen you to be a people for His treasured possession, out of all the peoples who are on the face of the earth. It was not because you were more in number than any other people that the LORD set His love on you and chose you, for you were the fewest of all peoples, but it is because the LORD loves you and is keeping the oath that He swore to your fathers, that the LORD has brought you out with a mighty hand and redeemed you from the house of slavery, from the hand of Pharaoh king of Egypt. (Deuteronomy 7:6–8)

God didn't select Israel because of their power or might. He didn't pick them out of the crowd because they had earned special recognition. God chose them out of love—a love they didn't deserve.

As we study the Book of Hosea, you will notice this theme running throughout the narrative: God loves us with a relentless love, even though we can never merit such a love.

God loves us with a relentless love, even though we can never merit such a love.

Moses reminded the people how God rescued them from Pharaoh, king of Egypt. The Lord brought them to the land of Canaan, where He instructed them to destroy the wicked, idolatrous people living in that land. On a very grand scale, He made this group of ragtag slaves from Egypt an object lesson of what it looks like to follow Yahweh, the one true God.

During the reigns of the judges and of Kings David and Solomon, the nation of Israel was united. After Solomon died, his son Rehoboam became king, but ten of the twelve tribes of Israel rebelled against him. They seceded from the nation and followed a new king—Jeroboam. While King Jeroboam ruled over the northern nation, called Israel (or Ephraim, after its leading tribe), King Rehoboam reigned over the southern nation of Judah (also named for its leading tribe).

Jeroboam immediately realized that it would be difficult to retain his rule if his people returned to the temple in Jerusalem (which was in Judah) for the feasts God had commanded. So Jeroboam erected golden calves, appointed his own priests, and told his people, "You have gone up to Jerusalem long enough. Behold your gods, O Israel, who brought you up out of the land of Egypt" (1 Kings 12:28). He wanted them to stay home and under his rule. Soon, the people of Israel began worshiping these idols, along with Canaanite gods such as Baal and Asherah.

Over the years, the Lord sent prophets like Elijah and Elisha to get the people's attention. He allowed world powers to threaten the nation to bring them to repentance. But Israel continued its idolatrous ways.

So God sent Hosea. The prophet Hosea opens his book by telling us that the word of the Lord came to him "in the days of Jeroboam the son of Joash, king of Israel" (Hosea 1:1). Not related to the first King Jeroboam who crafted the golden calves, this Jeroboam—Jeroboam II—became king in 793 BC, about a century and a half later, and reigned over the nation for forty-one years (see 2 Kings 14:23). God gave Jeroboam II victory in battle, and during his long and prosperous reign, he recovered much land from Israel's enemies.

Unfortunately, the Israelites did not respond with faithfulness and devotion to the God who provided prosperity. Instead, wealth and affluence brought "moral degeneracy, social evils, and religious corruption."[1] The prophet Amos, who lived and prophesied about the same time as Hosea, spoke of Israel's mistreatment of the poor, perversion of justice, incestuous behavior, and their profaning of God's holy name (see Amos 2:7–8).

Although Israel's love story began with God tenderly calling this small and insignificant nation to be His own, asking only for faithfulness in return, the people rejected God's ways. Like a wife who left a loving husband for another man, Israel went off in search of other lovers.

HOSEA AND GOMER

Years after John and I got back together, he confessed the trepidation he felt over our reunion. Because I had rejected him once, he feared I might do it again. In fact, even when our relationship had grown strong and he decided to propose marriage, he didn't get down on one knee and offer a formal proposal. Instead, he merely hinted he would like to marry me. He feared a refusal and that I would, in his words, "run off to the circus again."

Hosea must have had even graver concerns when God told him who he was to marry. The prophet tells us God's message:

> When the LORD first spoke through Hosea, the LORD said to Hosea, "Go, take to yourself a wife of whoredom and have children of whoredom, for the land commits great whoredom by forsaking the LORD." (Hosea 1:2)

God yearned for His people to repent and return to Him, so He sent a prophet whose very name means "salvation." He sent Hosea. And the Lord not only gave Hosea a message for the people, He also instructed this prophet to live out the message in a very public and personal object lesson.

Can you imagine Hosea's reaction to this instruction? "Really, God? Marry a *prostitute*? Uh . . . I'm not sure I can get on board with this plan. I mean, this woman has already been unfaithful. How can You guarantee she'll stay faithful to me?"

Scripture doesn't record Hosea's misgivings though. Instead, it tells us, "So he went and took Gomer, the daughter of Diblaim" (Hosea 1:3a). The prophet acted in obedience to the Lord and married Gomer.

CULTIC PROSTITUTION

Scripture gives little information about this woman with the name that makes me think of a mechanic on an old sitcom. (Poor girl!) She may have lived the life of a common prostitute, but it is also possible that she practiced her harlotry at a Canaanite shrine. The high places of Israel included altars to the pagan gods Baal and Asherah. Adoration of these deities involved intercourse with cult prostitutes as a way to ensure the fertility of the worshiper's fields and animals. When the Israelites adopted these false gods, they also embraced the local pagan practices, utterly ignoring God's laws.[2] Some scholars think that the common practice of the day had young Canaanite girls serve at these shrines before they married. Gomer may have been forced into this kind of life.

God instructed Hosea to show love to a woman "of whoredom" because God continued to love the nation of Israel, even though it had committed "great whoredom by forsaking the LORD" (v. 2). Hosea's personal life illustrated God's persistent love for an unfaithful people.

This Old Testament story of a faithful prophet with a wayward wife also depicts Christ's love for us. As New Testament believers, we are Christ's Bride (see Revelation 19:7–9). To be clear, He did not pick us out of the crowd because of our beauty, talent, or achievements. He didn't choose us because we sought Him first. Stuck in our sin, we acted unfaithfully. We rejected Him. Yet Christ loved the Church enough to sacrifice Himself for her to make her clean (see Ephesians 5:25–27).

We can also take Hosea's unusual life lesson to a personal level. Have you ever doubted God's love for you because you felt undeserving? I know I have. No, I haven't played the part of prostitute like Gomer, but sometimes, I have looked for love and recognition in places other than my loving Father. I've abandoned trust in the Lord and instead put my faith in the gods of success and accomplishment. Maybe you, too, have strayed from God's goodness, looked for love in the wrong places, and intentionally walked away from Christ.

God loves us because He loves us. Our imperfection, shame, and failure cannot diminish His relentless love.

Gomer's story reminds me that God loves me no matter how messy my life is or how imperfect my character. Gomer's life with Hosea teaches us that God doesn't love us because of our perfection—she had violated God's Law. God doesn't love us because we have a sparkling reputation—Gomer had lived the life of a harlot. God doesn't love us because of our accomplishments—Gomer's résumé was anything but impressive.

God loves us because He loves us. Our imperfection, shame, and failure cannot diminish His relentless love.

HOSEA'S UNIQUE MARRIAGE

God's instructions to Hosea to marry a "wife of whoredom" do not extend to us. God's Word warns us to avoid adulterers because involvement with them can lead to emotional pain and spiritual death (see Proverbs 2:16–18). It also cautions us to choose godly spouses and not "be unequally yoked with unbelievers" (2 Corinthians 6:14). God asked His prophet to love an unchaste woman as a living sign of His unwavering love for unfaithful Israel, but He does not ask the same of us.

HOSEA AND GOMER'S CHILDREN

It isn't long before Hosea and Gomer's household is overrun by little ones:

> So he went and took Gomer, the daughter of Diblaim, and she conceived and bore him a son.
> And the LORD said to him, "Call his name Jezreel, for in just a little while I will punish the house of Jehu for the blood of Jezreel, and I will put an end to the kingdom of the house of Israel. And on that day I will break the bow of Israel in the Valley of Jezreel."

She conceived again and bore a daughter. And the LORD said to him, "Call her name No Mercy, for I will no more have mercy on the house of Israel, to forgive them at all. But I will have mercy on the house of Judah, and I will save them by the LORD their God. I will not save them by bow or by sword or by war or by horses or by horsemen."

When she had weaned No Mercy, she conceived and bore a son. And the LORD said, "Call his name Not My People, for you are not My people, and I am not your God." (Hosea 1:3–9)

Imagine for a moment that you have recently married a nice Hebrew man and moved next door to Hosea and Gomer. You have heard of the birth of their baby, and you pop over to bring some lentil soup.

You knock on the door, and a boy who appears to be about five years old opens the door a crack.

"Hi, little guy! I'm Rebekah from next door. I have a pot of soup here for your mum. Can I come in?"

The boy opens the door wider; you enter and set the soup pot on the table. On a bed in the back corner of the room, Gomer nurses the baby. "Don't get up, dear," you continue. "I heard about your joyous news, and I thought I'd come to help out a bit."

You notice the boy who let you in and a smaller girl gazing at the pot of soup. You offer, "How about if I scoop up some soup for the new baby's big brother and sister?"

Gomer mumbles her thanks, and the boy finds some pottery bowls on a nearby shelf. As you ladle broth and vegetables into the bowls, you smile and ask the little ones, "So what are your names?"

"Jezreel."

"Lo-Ruhamah."

Your hand stops mid pour. What strange names! But trying not to appear critical or disapproving, you continue doling out lunch. You call over to Gomer, "And what did you name the baby?"

"Lo-Ammi."

"Oh. That's . . . nice," you reply with a forced smile. You think, *Poor kids.*

Many people probably shook their heads over these unusual monikers. God had continued sending His warning to Israel by assigning symbolic names to Hosea's children.

Jezreel. God gave the firstborn son a name that would have shocked the neighbors. To our ears, Jezreel is just another funny-sounding Hebrew name, but to the people of God, it would have been like giving an innocent baby a name like *Dachau* or *Auschwitz.*

Although the kings of Israel lived in the rich and fertile valley of Jezreel, it became a place of much bloodshed. The violence began when wicked King Ahab killed Naboth to get Naboth's vineyard in Jezreel (see 1 Kings 21 and continuing). To punish Ahab for this murder, the Lord destroyed Ahab's dynasty by anointing Jehu as the new king. Jehu, in an effort to establish his reign and destroy any fight for the crown, ordered the deaths of Ahab's seventy sons and had their heads piled up at the gates of the city of Jezreel (see 2 Kings 10). Then he had all of Ahab's supporters murdered—"all his great men and his close friends and his priests, until he left him none remaining" (2 Kings 10:11). The Lord had chosen Jehu, but Jehu had overstepped his authority and disobeyed God's Law.

Now, about fifty years later, God spoke a message to "the house of Jehu" (Hosea 1:4) by naming Hosea's son *Jezreel.* God would punish Jehu's dynasty for the unnecessary bloodshed. Although the kingdom of Israel remained in the hands of Jehu's descendants for five generations, the dynasty eventually ended with the assassination of Zechariah, son of Jeroboam II, and great-great-grandson of Jehu.

No Mercy. Next, Gomer gave birth to a daughter. Gomer may have wanted to give her little girl a beautiful name in the Hebrew tradition, such as Sarah or Rachel, but God assigned the name *No Mercy.* The original Hebrew name, *Lo-Ruhamah,* is derived from the Hebrew words *lo,* meaning "not,"[3] and *racham,* which means "to love deeply" or "to have compassion."[4]

Can you imagine going through life with the name *Not Loved*? Yet God used this name to alert the Israelites that their time of mercy would soon end. He would no longer overlook their idolatry and unfaithfulness.

Not My People. After little No Mercy was weaned (probably around age 3), Gomer conceived again and gave birth to another son. God assigned this baby the Hebrew name *Lo-ammi*. *Ammi* means "people" or "nation."[5] Through this name, God signaled the end of His covenant relationship with His chosen people. He told them, "You are not My people, and I am not your God" (Hosea 1:9).

Ever since He had rescued them from Egypt, God had set the nation of Israel apart as a treasured possession (see Exodus 19:5–6). They existed as a distinct people blessed by God for as long as they obeyed God's voice and kept His covenant. But He warned them:

> The LORD will bring upon you all the evil things . . . if you transgress the covenant of the LORD your God, which He commanded you, and go and serve other gods and bow down to them. Then the anger of the LORD will be kindled against you, and you shall perish quickly from off the good land that He has given to you. (Joshua 23:15–16)

God's patience had endured for centuries, but the names of Hosea's children indicated His tolerance had finally expired. Yahweh would punish Israel's rulers for their unjust killings. He would no longer show the people mercy. In fact, they would no longer continue as His people.

SPIRITUAL WHIPLASH

When our daughter was about five years old, my husband told her an abridged version of the story of how we met. In telling of my unceremonious rejection of him, John said, "Your mom dropped me like a hot potato."

Anna turned to me and asked, "Why did you drop Daddy like a boiled potato?"

Ignoring the cooking method, I explained, "At first, I didn't realize what a good thing I had. It took me awhile to recognize I couldn't find anyone better than your daddy."

During that year of singing and travel, my world expanded and I matured. When I returned home, I clearly saw that I had been a fool to not attempt a long-distance relationship with this cute, funny, gentle, and loving man. Was it too late? Surely by now, this wonderful person had found someone else and moved on. He wouldn't want to try again with the person who had mashed his heart like a potato.

The Israelites probably experienced a similar apprehension. God said He would put an end to the kingdom of the house of Israel, withdraw His mercy, and reject them as His people (see Hosea 1:4–9). That sounds final. Absolute. Irrevocable.

However, immediately after Hosea tells of God's judgment, he offers hope:

> Yet the number of the children of Israel shall be like the sand of the sea, which cannot be measured or numbered. And in the place where it was said to them, "You are not My people," it shall be said to them, "Children of the living God." And the children of Judah and the children of Israel shall be gathered together, and they shall appoint for themselves one head. And they shall go up from the land, for great shall be the day of Jezreel.
>
> Say to your brothers, "You are My people," and to your sisters, "You have received mercy." (Hosea 1:10–2:1)

This feels like spiritual whiplash. In one verse, God says one thing, and in the next, He speaks the opposite. Sudden contrasts abound in the Book of Hosea. At times we may scratch our heads in confusion, but we can also uncover beauty in these God-given reversals.

I thank God for my own personal reversals. I never expected John to come back into my life. But when he called, asking for the phone numbers of my friends, I recognized that he hadn't moved on yet and I had better try a reconciliation before he did. Slowly, we rebuilt our friendship. John proceeded warily at first, but in the end, our relationship was restored.

God also was willing to restore the relationship with Israel. He reached out to His chosen people with a word of hope. He moved from harsh words to loving expressions. From Law to Gospel. Yes, the Israelites would suffer punishment for their disobedience and unfaithfulness. As a just and righteous God, He couldn't overlook sin. But later, He would forgive and restore.

God reached out to His chosen people with a word of hope. He moved from harsh words to loving expressions.

Let's look at each of Hosea's contrasts, according to the names of his children.

Jezreel. God moved from words of punishment for the bloodshed in Jezreel (see Hosea 1:4–5) to reconciliation and hope: "And the children of Judah and the children of Israel shall be gathered together, and they shall appoint for themselves one head. And they shall go up from the land, for great shall be the day of Jezreel" (v. 11). Hosea presented the fulfillment of God's promise to Abraham that the Savior of the world would come through Abraham's descendants (see Genesis 22:18). The prophet looked forward to the day when Israel and Judah would be reunited and have one king—when all would worship the Messiah, the true King of the people of God.

Although the valley of Jezreel had a reputation for violence, God made a play on the original meaning of the name, "God will sow." He declared that the people would "go up" from the land. The Hebrew word for "go up" is *alah*, which can mean "to go up, ascend" or "to spring up, grow, shoot forth."[6] Instead of destruction, "the future age in [God's] kingdom will be a time for planting and growing, fruit-bearing and harvesting."[7] The seed of the Gospel will bear fruit.

No Mercy. At the birth of Hosea's daughter, God spoke harsh words: "I will no more have mercy on the house of Israel" (Hosea 1:6); but in chapter 2, God offered hope: "Say . . . to your sisters, 'You have received mercy'" (2:1). Near the end of the Book of Hosea, God said, "How can I give you up, O Ephraim? How can I hand you over, O Israel? . . . My heart recoils within Me; My compassion grows warm and tender" (11:8). With these words, God revealed His loving, compassionate nature. As a loving Father, He must punish His child to bring him back, but we know that God cannot totally abandon His people.

Not My People. Hosea's second son received the name *Lo-Ammi* because God declared, "You are not My people, and I am not your God" (Hosea 1:9). If the people of Hosea's day cared for Yahweh at all, these words of rejection must have made their hearts sink. Since Abraham, the Israelites had existed as the treasured possession of the one true God. What would happen to them if Yahweh no longer cherished and protected them? Thankfully, God promised restoration: "In the place where it was said to them, 'You are not My people,' it shall be said to them, 'Children of the living God'" (v. 10). Whew! The relationship would one day be renewed.

LIVE LIKE YOU'RE LOVED

So what does the story of a faithful prophet and his wayward wife have to do with us? How can the ancient account of a prostitute with a funny name change our twenty-first-century lives?

Gomer's tale and Hosea's words remind us all that God doesn't dole out His mercy based on our perfection. He doesn't distribute His love depending on our worthiness. Nothing we can do would make the Father love us any more than He already does. Nothing we have done can diminish His affection.

Nothing we can do would make the Father love us any more than He already does. Nothing we have done can diminish His affection.

HOSEA IN THE NEW TESTAMENT

Did you know that the New Testament quotes Hosea more than any other minor prophet?[8] Paul quoted Hosea 1:10 in his Letter to the Romans: "And in the very place where it was said to them, 'You are not My people,' there they will be called 'sons of the living God'" (Romans 9:26).

Paul tells us the good news of belonging that Hosea shared with Israel also extends to us. He "contends that if God could restore the 10 tribes of Israel . . . who had abandoned Him, He can also call Gentiles to be the recipients of His mercy."[9] The apostle Peter also echoes, "Once you were not a people, but now you are God's people; once you had not received mercy, but now you have received mercy" (1 Peter 2:10). Because of Christ's death, which wipes out all our sin, we all can be God's people. We can all receive mercy. We can all belong.

When I am reminded of this good news, my heart fills with relief and hope. When I have neglected my relationship with God or snapped at my husband, God does not reject me. When I've ignored a friend in need or let selfishness govern how I spend my money, the Lord doesn't give up on me. I experience the consequences of my behavior. But even as the Father disciplines me, He still calls me His beloved child.

Let the truth of Hosea seep into your heart. When you have messed up, when you are certain God could never forgive what you've done, remember God's words to His wayward nation: "Say to your brothers, 'You are My people,' and to your sisters, 'You have received mercy'" (Hosea 2:1). Repeat these words to your own hurting heart and to your brothers and sisters in Christ. Remember that you are baptized—forgiven, rescued, and saved for eternity.

When we trust in Jesus' death and resurrection as the solution to all our sins, we can live like we're loved. As God's beloved children, we are His people. God's relentless love calls us His own.

CHAPTER TWO

A Relentless Love Story

Steven stepped into Theresa's office and set a can of cola on her desk. "Not trying to bother you. Just bringing you a diet cola," he said as he held up his hands surrender-style and backed out of the room.

Although he had just arrived at the company, my brother, Steven, could tell that the financial controller didn't think much of him. The way she frowned and wrinkled her brow when she saw him made it obvious she did not like the new hire.

Knowing he would need to work closely with this woman (and knowing her drink preferences), Steven decided to make a peace offering in the form of a diet cola instead of an olive branch. Meanwhile, Theresa wondered, *Who does this guy think he is?* When Steven gave a presentation to the whole company during his very first week on the job, she thought, *What a show-off.*

After a month of morning cola visits, Theresa told her mom about the guy at work who brought her a cola every day. "I think he likes you," her mother said. Theresa wasn't convinced. And even if Steven did like her, she still didn't like him.

But she did like diet cola.

A couple of months later, a group of people from work went out after office hours. Steven happened to sit next to Theresa at a round high-top table. When the band started playing, Steven started "dancing" in his seat. Seeing him smiling and bouncing to the beat, Theresa thought,

Maybe this guy isn't all bad. After a few more weeks of daily colas, he asked her out, and Theresa agreed. A Mexican restaurant that served pizza and used taxidermy as decor made their first date memorable.

When Steven hosted a Fourth of July party at his home, he introduced his family to the girl he was dating. At last, my sister and I got to meet the mystery woman we had heard so much about, and we immediately loved Theresa's sense of humor. Certain she would be an asset to the family, we tried to convince her that our brother was "highly trainable." (Theresa didn't know what to make of that.)

The work romance blossomed into something more and continued even after Theresa moved on to a new job. Eventually, they were married in a lovely restaurant on Chicago's Navy Pier, and they have been together for years. Their relationship has survived work-related challenges and health problems.

And relentless diet cola started it all.

God's Relentless Love Pursues

Hosea 2

MEMORY VERSE

And I will betroth you to Me forever. I will betroth you
to Me in righteousness and in justice,
in steadfast love and in mercy.

Hosea 2:19

How did the love of your life pursue you? Or how did your best friend become more than a casual acquaintance?

My brother plied his now-wife with diet soft drinks. Maybe your boyfriend used flowers. Maybe your best friend became your best friend because she sat next to you at every Wednesday-morning Bible study.

Scripture doesn't give us any details of Hosea and Gomer's courtship. But can you imagine a young prophet showing up at your door and saying, "God told me to marry you. Get your things. Let's head down to the justice of the peace and get it done"? (That would have been even stranger than a letter signed in blue crayon!) It doesn't sound particularly romantic, but perhaps it happened much that way. After all, in Bible times, marriages were usually arranged by the parents of the couple and were not based on romantic love. Plus, men did not seek out unchaste women as marriage prospects. If a Jewish dating app had featured Gomer, most likely no one would have tried to connect with her because of her bad reputation. So when Hosea came calling, Gomer probably said yes.

Although chapter 1 of Hosea doesn't reveal details of Hosea's courtship of Gomer, chapter 2 describes God's courtship of Israel. In his commentary on Hosea, author Douglas Stuart writes:

> In this allegory, Yahweh "courts" Israel in two senses. He takes Israel to court in the accusation of a crime—adultery. But as the passage unfolds, it is clear from the outset . . . that the actual purpose will be to "court" Israel in the sense of inviting her back to faithfulness after she has done penance for her sin.[10]

Chapter 2 of Hosea takes the form of a lawsuit, alternating between accusations and judgment, damning evidence and punishing sentences. Israel plays the defendant charged with adultery. Yahweh is the plaintiff—the wronged husband. But He also acts as the prosecutor, the judge, and the jury.[11]

HEBREW POETRY

Chapter 2 of Hosea has a dramatic shift of style. While chapter 1 presents the story of Hosea and Gomer in prose, chapter 2 switches to poetry. As you read Hosea 2, you may not think it sounds poetic because it doesn't have rhyming words or a predictable rhythm. However, the distinctive feature of Hebrew poetry is parallelism—two lines of text that are parallel in meaning. We can see three main types of parallelism in Hosea 2:

1. The second line restates the meaning of the first line:
   "I will hedge up her way with thorns,
   and I will build a wall against her" (v. 6).
2. The second line contrasts with the first line:
   "[Israel] went after her lovers
   and forgot Me, declares the LORD" (v. 13).
3. The second line develops the thought of the first line:
   "Upon her children also I will have no mercy,
   because they are children of whoredom" (v. 4).

This parallelism helps us understand the message. If we have difficulty understanding the first line, the second can clarify.[12]

FIRST ACCUSATION

Israel Pursued Other Lovers

The trial begins in an unusual way. The Prosecutor calls on the defendant's children to give evidence against their mother. He says, "Plead with your mother, plead." The prosecutor hopes the children will be able to convince their mother to "put away her whoring from her face, and her adultery from between her breasts" (Hosea 2:2). If this accusation addresses Gomer as well as Israel, it may indicate that Hosea's wife wore the makeup and jewelry of a prostitute. Gomer—and Israel—made their unfaithfulness obvious to everyone around them.

God continues the charges:

> For their mother has played the whore;
>> she who conceived them has acted shamefully.
> For she said, "I will go after my lovers,
>> who give me my bread and my water,
>> my wool and my flax, my oil and my drink." (Hosea 2:5)

The Judge accuses Israel of prostitution. In fact, Israel chased after her lovers instead of following the profession's usual custom of simply allowing clients to come to her. Israel actively sought out other lovers.

Who are those lovers? The gods of Canaan: Baal, Asherah, and Asheroth. During the reign of Jeroboam II, Baal-worship wasn't officially sanctioned but was widely practiced. In what we call syncretism, Israel gave glory to Yahweh but added worship of the Canaanite gods for good measure. Perhaps they wanted to fit in with the local culture. Maybe they wanted to hedge their bets. They probably thought, *What could it hurt? We don't want to offend any powerful beings. And if worshiping one god brings blessings, worshiping two or three should bring even more.* But Yahweh had commanded, "You shall have no other gods before Me" (Exodus 20:3).

How will the Judge respond? The usual sentence for adultery was stoning (see Deuteronomy 22:23–24), but God announced a sentence of exile. He declared, "I will hedge up her way with thorns, and I will build a wall against her" (Hosea 2:6). The images of hedges and walls predict a time when other nations would overpower Israel and take her captive. God plans to use this captivity to call His wayward nation back to Himself. In exile, Israel will not have access to the Canaanite gods. After the time of exile, Yahweh hopes she will say, "I will go and return to my first husband, for it was better for me then than now" (v. 7). The verb *return* communicates repentance, but the word also indicates return from exile.[13] The sentence of banishment from the Promised Land seems cruel, but God knows it will bring some of His chosen people back to their senses. They will realize they were better off with Yahweh than with counterfeit gods.[14]

If I stood trial in God's court, the Prosecutor could bring charges of syncretism against me too. My worship of other gods may not look as overt as that of the Israelites, but like them, I allow my culture to influence me. Without constant vigilance, I can easily slip into worshiping the gods of materialism and success. I chase after them for the things I desire: comfort and recognition. Yes, God gives me blessings, but if I don't receive everything I think I deserve, I begin worshiping at the altar of productivity and the shrine of busyness. Syncretism in our modern world may not look like multiple idols in our living room; rather, it may appear as too many demands on our schedule, preventing us from spending time in God's Word. It may look like too many items in our closets, taking away our attention from the God who provided them.

Sometimes God's relentless love looks like punishment. When He blocks my way from getting something I desperately want, I gripe and complain and go looking for it somewhere else. But when God builds a wall, He does it in love. The wall stops me from pursuing harmful things. Walls prevent me from running from His love and grace. The doors of opportunities slamming in my face don't signify a cruel, punitive God but indicate the desire of a loving Father to keep me close.

The doors of opportunities slamming in my face don't signify a cruel, punitive God but indicate the desire of a loving Father to keep me close.

SECOND ACCUSATION

Israel Credits Her Other Lovers with Providing for Her

The Prosecutor stands again and points His finger at Israel:

> She did not know
> that it was I who gave her
> the grain, the wine, and the oil,
> and who lavished on her silver and gold,
> which they used for Baal. (Hosea 2:8)

This adulterous wife keeps running after other lovers, looking to them instead of her loving husband to supply her needs.

In effect, God—the wronged husband—testifies, "She didn't even realize that I had provided for her needs all along. I fed her. I clothed her. I arranged for her celebrations even though she didn't include Me in them. I even made her prosperous, supplied her with silver and gold. And what does she do? She used these very gifts to make images of her other lovers!" It was as if my brother Steven had overheard Theresa talking with a co-worker, giving credit to the night janitor for her daily diet colas.

In Hosea 2, the Judge has heard enough and issues His sentence in the form of three punishments:

Agricultural failure and famine. Since Israel didn't recognize that the blessings of food and clothing came from Yahweh, He will take them away. Israel talked about "*my* bread and *my* water, *my* wool and *my* flax, *my* oil and *my* drink" (Hosea 2:5, emphasis added) and gave credit for those gifts to Baal. Now God says, "I will take back *My* grain in its time, and *My* wine in its season, and I will take away *My* wool and *My* flax" (v. 9, emphasis added).

All the blessings belonged to God in the first place. And *He* gave them to His beloved.

Shame and nakedness. The Judge issues another punishment: the shame of Israel's adultery will be exposed. Yahweh declares, "Now I will uncover her lewdness in the sight of her lovers, and no one shall rescue her out of My hand" (Hosea 2:10). The word *uncover* in Hebrew is *galah,* which means not only "to uncover" but "to go into exile."[15] God will take away His protection. Enemies will overpower the nation and take the people into captivity. The nations around her will gawk at her shame. Because of her unfaithfulness, she will be disgraced.

Loss of feasts and festivals. But that's not enough punishment, the Judge declares. In addition, "I will put an end to all her mirth, her feasts, her new moons, her Sabbaths, and all her appointed feasts" (Hosea 2:11). This was more than saying, "You're grounded! No parties for you this weekend!" The feasts, Sabbaths, and festivals were a source of Israel's identity. God had instituted annual celebrations of Passover, Pentecost, and the Feast of Booths. The Law of Moses directed priests to make a special sacrifice at every new moon to dedicate the new month to the Lord (see Numbers 28:11). And the Ten Commandments instructed the people of Israel to devote one day of every week to God (see Exodus 20:8).

Why would Yahweh demolish the very system He had instituted? Because instead of using these celebrations to worship God, the people burned offerings to Baal (see Hosea 2:13). Picture a faithful husband going to work every day to provide lavishly for his wife but coming home to a party his wife has thrown for other men. Through the lit windows of his home, he sees her other lovers enjoying expensive cheeses and appetizers, costly merlots and chardonnays. The food and drink he worked for and gave in love were now being enjoyed by others.

I can *tsk-tsk* Israel, but I have often treated God in much the same way. I tend to view my blessings as my own—things obtained through worship at the altars of busyness and success. At times, I've overlooked the fact that everything I have comes from the God who loves me and longs to provide for me. I've used the blessings He has given for my own pleasure. I've catered to the gods of achievement, comfort, and recreation and ignored my Beloved's invitation to spend time with Him.

THIRD ACCUSATION

Israel Has Forgotten Yahweh

The Judge pounds His gavel. "Order in the court!" The murmuring stops and the Judge asks, "Are there any more charges?"

The Lord, as Prosecutor and Husband, offers one final charge:

[She] adorned herself with her ring and jewelry,
and went after her lovers
and forgot Me, declares the LORD. (Hosea 2:13)

How can a marriage continue if the wife has completely forgotten her husband? Israel became so preoccupied with chasing after other lovers that she forgot about her most important relationship. Surely this means the end of the marriage. The courtroom awaits the Judge's announcement of the dissolution of the marriage and the sentence of death by stoning. If the bride has abandoned her husband and prostituted herself, she deserves the most severe punishment.

YAHWEH COURTS ISRAEL

But Yahweh surprises everyone in the courtroom. Instead of punishing the unfaithful wife, He says:

Therefore, behold, I will allure her,
and bring her into the wilderness,
and speak tenderly to her.
And there I will give her her vineyards
and make the Valley of Achor a door of hope.
And there she shall answer as in the days of her youth,
as at the time when she came out of the land of Egypt.
(Hosea 2:14–15)

As a wronged husband, God has every right to turn His back on the relationship. She has forgotten Him; He could simply forget her. Yet He decides to do the opposite. He will romance her and win her back. In the Hebrew, *pathath*, the word translated here as "allure," also means "to seduce, persuade, and entice." "Speak tenderly" comes from the Hebrew words *dabar*, "to speak, declare, or promise," and *leb*, "the heart, soul, and emotions." This expression is used in courtship and in winning back love.[16] God will not give up on Israel. Instead, He will court her, pursue her, and win her heart once again.

I enjoy a good love story. But if I were watching a film portraying the romantic drama of Hosea and Gomer, of Yahweh and Israel, I would want to shout at the screen to warn Hosea, to warn Yahweh, to dump that wild woman. I mean, "Don't you see what's going to happen? Are you a glutton for punishment? Do you want her to stomp on your heart again?"

Yet God ignores logic, disregards the possibility of rejection, and pursues His beloved once again.

To regain her affection, the Lord arranges time alone with His beloved. He will bring her into the wilderness because, when Israel was young, the wilderness forged her relationship with Yahweh. The wilderness may not sound like a lovely romantic setting (I'd prefer a luxury hotel suite with rose petals on the bed and mints on the pillows), but it isolated Israel from her false lovers. The nation needed that seclusion when leaving Egypt with its false gods and heathen practices, and it needed it in Hosea's time. Without the distraction of the Canaanite gods, Israel might once again recognize her true love—Yahweh.

What grace. Even after we've turned away from God, spent time with other loves, and forgotten about spending time with Him, He still pursues us.

What grace. Even after we've turned away from God, spent time with other loves, and forgotten about spending time with Him, He still pursues us. He speaks tender words of love and constantly assures us that we still belong to Him. And when we experience "wilderness" times in our lives, may we see them as opportunities to grow in our relationship with the One who loves us deeply. I don't know about you, but when my life progresses according to my plans, I tend to suffer spiritual amnesia. However, when health problems, financial setbacks, or relationship struggles show up at my door, I remember my desperate need for God. I turn back to Him, asking for relief from my pain, and in the process, the One who has patiently waited for me to come to Him renews our relationship.

VALLEY OF ACHOR

In Hosea 2:15, God says He will "make the Valley of Achor a door of hope." When the Israelites first entered the Promised Land and defeated the city of Jericho, God commanded that all the silver and gold recovered from that city be dedicated to Him. However, Achan secretly took some of the dedicated things for himself. Because of this sin, Israel experienced defeat in battle, and when Joshua sought the Lord, God revealed Achan as the cause of the loss. As punishment, Joshua and all of Israel stoned Achan and burned all his belongings in the Valley of Achor—which came to mean "trouble."

However, here in Hosea, God declares that the Valley of Achor (or the Valley of Trouble) will become a door of hope. The Lord promises that after a time of punishment, He will restore Israel's relationship with Him. "The exile—trouble because of Israel's disobedience—will be for some of the people of Israel an entrance to hope, because the Lord will use it to lead them to repentance."[17]

MY HUSBAND

Court adjourns. The Judge dismisses the trial because the wronged Husband has, in effect, dropped the charges. He takes on the project of winning back His wife's affection. Yahweh tenderly pursues Israel. Although He knows she won't come back to Him without a time of exile and separation, He confidently declares that she will return:

> And in that day, declares the LORD, you will call Me "My Husband," and no longer will you call Me "My Baal." For I will remove the names of the Baals from her mouth, and they shall be remembered by name no more. (Hosea 2:16–17)

In Hebrew, both of the words translated as "My Husband" and "My Baal" can mean "husband." The first word, *'iysh*, refers to a man, husband, or marriage partner. The second, *Ba'ally*, brings more of the meaning of lord, master, and the legal rights of a husband over a wife. But the real miracle will be that Israel will no longer call Baal her husband; instead, she will return to Yahweh and identify Him as her marriage partner. In fact, there will come a time when Israel completely forgets about her false lovers. Baal, neglected and forgotten, will be so out of mind that God's people won't even remember the false god's name.

IN THAT DAY

God uses the phrase "in that day" three times in Hosea 2. "That day" refers to the time when God will come as Savior and Judge. First, Jesus fulfilled the prophet's words when He came to earth to redeem His Bride. Then, eternal blessings of peace and abundance will be fully realized when Jesus comes again in glory.[18] With the phrase "in that day," God looks forward in time.

When Israel finally comes to her senses, God promises betrothal. He speaks directly to His beloved:

> And I will betroth you to Me forever. I will betroth you to Me in righteousness and in justice, in steadfast love and in mercy. I will betroth you to Me in faithfulness. And you shall know the Lord. (Hosea 2:19–20)

Like our modern engagements, a betrothal in Bible times was a promise to marry. But unlike modern engagements, with their social media-worthy proposals, parents usually brought the two young people together. Instead of giving the bride-to-be a diamond ring, the groom would pay a bride price to her family to compensate them for the loss of their daughter. A formal betrothal ceremony made the union as legally binding as the wedding ritual (which normally took place about one year later).

Yahweh also promises His beloved that this betrothal would be forever. He assures her of His faithfulness. He promises to betroth her in righteousness, justice, steadfast love, and mercy. These four qualities can be understood as the bride price.[19] This union will cost God something in the currency of unfailing love, undeserved mercy, and unearned righteousness.

God then promises that His betrothed will know the Lord. Before, Israel forgot Yahweh and gave herself to her other lovers, but in the future, she will again have an intimate relationship with the one true God.

As New Testament Christians, we are referred to in the Bible as Christ's Bride. However, we may live like we've forgotten this truth. Instead of following the God who loved us from the beginning, we turn to other pursuits, chase other interests. We love material goods, listen to the empty promises of the world, and all but forget the true God. Yet Christ came to this broken, dusty earth to be with us, to pursue us, and to call us back into relationship with Him.

> Christ loved the church and gave Himself up for her, that He might sanctify her, having cleansed her by the washing of water with the word, so that He might present the church to Himself in splendor, without spot or wrinkle or any such thing, that she might be holy and without blemish.
> (Ephesians 5:25–27)

The bride price for our righteousness cost Jesus His life as He suffered death on a cross. Perfectly sinless and absolutely faithful, He suffered the shame of mockery and nakedness to redeem His lewdly adulterous bride. He offered us His mercy, even when we didn't recognize our need for it. All this He gave so we could know Him intimately.

LIVE LIKE YOU'RE LOVED

When I was a young teenager, I saw a tract that pictured Judgment Day as a court setting. Like the court scene in Hosea, presenting Israel's crimes of unfaithfulness, this tract's cartoon drawings pictured one person before God as judge. All of the defendant's sins played on a movie screen above the Judge. This idea terrified me because not only did it make me think I would relive all my worst mistakes, but, according to the tract, everyone else on earth would see the replay of my door-slamming argument with my mother, the cigarette I smoked at a Girl Scout campout, my murderous thoughts toward the girl who got the high school honor I felt I deserved. Of course, all these years later, the film of my sins would be much longer and more horrifying. The movie might not be as X-rated as Gomer's, but it would certainly be a long double feature.

We can be thankful that the Bible tells us that Christians will never experience that dreadful courtroom scene. In the surprising reversal in Hosea, God as judge, jury, and plaintiff declared love and mercy to the accused instead of everlasting punishment and separation. In the same way, God declares to us, "There is therefore now no condemnation for those who are in Christ Jesus" (Romans 8:1). Instead of raising the gavel and convicting us of all our offenses and failings, Jesus got down from the bench and accepted our punishment for us. And when we trust in His atonement, Jesus courts us in a different way. Like Yahweh calling out to Israel, He says:

> Therefore, behold, I will allure her,
>   and bring her into the wilderness,
>   and speak tenderly to her. (Hosea 2:14)

Unbelievable. God desires me so much that He takes time to court me, romance me. He will arrange my circumstances so I spend more time with Him. He speaks gentle words of love.

When Steven attempted to charm Theresa, he did it with daily cans of cola. But he didn't make a big deal about it, didn't push his way into her space or her life. Similarly, Christ relentlessly courts me. He never forces

Himself on me, yet He always lets me know He is near, waiting for me to come to Him. He offers gifts of food and drink, clothing and shelter. He gives times of celebration. He offers the heady scent of lily of the valley, the azure shade of the twilight sky, the warm embrace of a friend, and the sweetness of a white-flesh nectarine as gifts of His love. He woos me, inviting me closer.

GIFTS OF ETERNAL NOURISHMENT

In Hosea 2:21–22, God promises "in that day," He will provide gifts of food—specifically grain and wine and oil. God may not always provide abundant food in our current lives, but He has provided for us generously in spiritual food. Jesus is the bread of life and He gives us Himself in the blessings of the bread and wine in the Lord's Supper.

But sometimes I am more enamored with the gifts than I am with the Giver. I give credit to the gods of hard work and productivity for my possessions and forget about the true Provider. That's when God may call me to spend more time alone with Him. Heartache, illness, or financial distress may enter my life so I realize my desperate need for the One who loves me. I finally become aware that the gods of productivity and materialism can't supply what I truly need and they never did.

Then I go to God's Word for His tender, loving words. I hear His Gospel message in Sunday sermons. I kneel to receive His Holy Meal and to be refreshed by it. The Holy Spirit may make me aware of my sinful ways, but He does this only so I repent, release the burden of sin, and hear Christ's loving words of forgiveness. I quiet my heart and hear Him say, "I have loved you with an everlasting love" (Jeremiah 31:3), and "You are precious in My eyes" (Isaiah 43:4). He whispers, "My steadfast love shall not depart from you" (Isaiah 54:10), and "[I] rejoice over you with gladness" (Zephaniah 3:17).

God primarily wants each one of us to call out to Him, "My Husband," and open our hearts to intimacy with Him.

Theologian Henri Nouwen wrote, "My true spiritual work is to let myself be loved, fully and completely."[20] We tend to think our spiritual work looks like a long to-do list: read three chapters of the Bible, spend at least ten minutes in prayer, serve on the church committee, and volunteer at the homeless shelter. These are all good and wonderful things, but God wants each of us to call out to Him, "My Husband," and open our hearts to intimacy with Him. The One who created us in His image and gave Himself up so we could live with Him forever asks us to simply receive His love. When we do that, all of the wonderful spiritual practices and works of service will come spontaneously.

God continually pursues you with His relentless love. Live like you're loved, fully and completely.

CHAPTER THREE

A RELENTLESS LOVE STORY

"Mary, have I got the guy for you!" Mary's friend had begun planning her wedding and had asked Mary to be a bridesmaid in it. She paired Mary with Dick as bridesmaid and groomsman because she had a feeling they would hit it off. Mary and Dick have been together ever since: two and a half years of dating and sixty-eight years of marriage!

Right after their wedding, Dick enlisted in the navy and they moved from Chicago, Illinois, to Norfolk, Virginia, for his years in the service. Dick spent long months away from his bride on a ship. Mary experienced loneliness in navy housing. "The hardest time," Mary said, "was after the birth of our first child. The baby arrived on a Friday, the doctors sent me home from the hospital on Sunday, and Dick left for a two-month stint on a ship on Monday. I had no idea what to do with this little baby and had no one to turn to for help." Other navy wives came and went, leaving for home after their husbands deployed. Mary thought of going home to Chicago, where she would have friends and family to support her, but she decided to stay because, in her words, "If I left, then Dick would be all alone when he got off the ship."

That selfless love defines their marriage. During Dick's two years in the navy, his ship routinely dumped live ammunition. Every time the sailors set out to Newfoundland for these missions, they faced the danger of not returning—after all, the live ammunition could explode. When I asked Mary how she felt about these missions, she said she hadn't even known about them at the time. Dick, not wanting to worry his bride, never gave details about his ship's missions.

After the navy, Dick and Mary returned to the Chicago area. Dick took a job with the gas company and they moved to the far western suburb of Aurora. Two more daughters arrived, and they had a happy family life.

The girls grew up, found jobs or got married, and life was good. Dick and Mary's house was the center of celebrations. When grandchildren arrived on the scene, Grandpa Dick was the life of the party. His immense love for the grandkids meant they could talk him into anything. When they begged to play a game that involved filled balloons, Grandpa said yes. Dick filled the balloons with water, shaving cream, chocolate syrup, and other equally messy things. He tied them to the clothesline in the backyard and had each grandkid sit under one of the balloons. When Dick popped the balloons, each child received a dousing of whatever the balloon held. They loved it! (Mary, on the other hand, did not share their enthusiasm for the game. She was stuck with bathing the chocolate-covered children.)

Not all of Dick and Mary's years were trouble-free. Hard times came to one of the daughters, and her whole family moved into their little house for twelve months. Over the years, they have housed many people who needed a bit of help. Their big hearts just can't say no.

When I asked them to share their secret for such a long and happy marriage, Mary said, "Trust each other." Marriage requires believing and depending on your spouse. Dick said, "Learn to bend a little." Isn't that often the practical definition of love? Don't always demand your own way.

GOD'S RELENTLESS LOVE REDEEMS

Hosea 3

MEMORY VERSE

And I said to her, "You must dwell as mine for many days."
Hosea 3:3

Dick and Mary's relentless love for each other has survived sixty-eight years of marriage so far. Amazing! But God's love for us endures forever. Even more amazing! As we examine Hosea and Gomer's story, we see that the Lord's love outlasts every obstacle and problem.

In chapter 2, we saw Yahweh's relationship with Israel, but chapter 3 brings us back to the Hosea-and-Gomer drama. After the birth of their three oddly named children, Hosea and Gomer's relationship splintered. At some point, Gomer left Hosea for another man. But even though Jewish law stated a man should not take back an adulterous wife (see Deuteronomy 24:1–4), God told Hosea to "Go again, love a woman who is loved by another man and is an adulteress, even as the LORD loves the children of Israel, though they turn to other gods and love cakes of raisins" (Hosea 3:1).

Because God wanted His people to see a tangible demonstration of how He never abandons those He loves, He asked Hosea to persist in his seemingly shattered marriage with Gomer. Imagine the scene when Yahweh gave Hosea new instructions:

Yahweh: Hosea!

Hosea: Yes, Lord?

Yahweh: Remember Gomer?

Hosea: How could I forget her? I took her out of her miserable life, married her, fathered her children, provided for her care, and what does she do? Leaves me for another man!

Yahweh: Yes, Hosea, that's all true. But I want you to find her, bring her back, and love her.

Hosea: You've got to be kidding! No offense, Lord, but I'm done with this relationship. No doubt You've heard the rumors: Hosea, man of God, marries a whore and can't even keep *her* at home. I mean, how would You feel if Your lover abandoned You for another? What if people dragged Your name through the mud?

Yahweh: I know exactly how you feel, Hosea. Israel, My beloved, has deserted Me and chased many other lovers. You feel your reputation has been dishonored? Look at how they treat My holy name! But I have not given up on My chosen people, and so I ask you not to abandon Gomer. Oh, and just one more thing.

Hosea: Yes, Lord?

Yahweh: You will need to buy Gomer back.

Hosea: Spend money to get what is already mine?

Yahweh: Yes, Hosea.

If I had been in Hosea's shoes, I know I would not have given in to God's request easily. I would have continued to argue that Gomer didn't have a faithful bone in her body. Surely God didn't need such a flawed individual as a sacred object lesson.

However, Scripture doesn't give any hint about a long, drawn-out exchange between Hosea and Yahweh. God says, "Go find Gomer," and Hosea obeys.

PROPHETIC SIGN-ACTS

Hosea couldn't leave his work at the office. Because of God's commands and instructions, his message and his personal life dovetailed. His life became a concrete illustration for the people of Israel.

In the Old Testament, God often used such prophetic sign-acts to demonstrate His message. God told Ezekiel to build a miniature siegeworks out of a brick and an iron griddle to warn the Israelites of the coming siege. Ezekiel then needed to lie on his side for 390 days to bear the penalty of the house of Israel and to symbolize the 390 years of punishment they would experience (see Ezekiel 4:1–7). Jeremiah had to wear straps and a yoke as a sign of the coming world domination of Nebuchadnezzar and the Babylonians (see Jeremiah 27:1–7). The Lord instructed Isaiah to walk around naked and barefoot for three years as a sign of the terrible troubles God would bring against Egypt and Cush (see Isaiah 20:1–4).[21]

Hosea's marriage to Gomer and the instruction to bring her back after she had deserted him were a living lesson of God's unwavering love for His people. This message extends to us: God wasn't discouraged by the high cost of our salvation. He sacrificed His own Son to bring us back to Him.

LIMITATIONS

When God gave the prophet the command to "Go again, *love* a woman who is loved by another man and is an adulteress" (Hosea 3:1, emphasis added), Hosea may have wanted to protest. "Okay, Lord. As a good and obedient prophet, I'll go and rescue her. I'll get her out of the mess she's gotten herself into. But love her? I promise to care for her and keep her safe, but I draw the line at love."

Yet Hosea obeyed God's command, however reluctantly. Once Hosea brought Gomer home, he gave her some parameters:

> You must dwell as mine for many days. You shall not play the
> whore, or belong to another man; so will I also be to you.
> (Hosea 3:3)

Hosea demonstrated his love by promising to be faithful to Gomer if she stopped giving herself to other lovers. God desired the same response from Israel, but His beloved had shown herself to be so unfaithful that He knew He needed to do something drastic. The next verse points to Israel's impending time of exile, when the Lord would isolate the nation from its false gods and deceitful loves:

> For the children of Israel shall dwell many days without king
> or prince, without sacrifice or pillar, without ephod or house-
> hold gods. (Hosea 3:4)

God outlines what He will take away in the hope that His people will return to Him. He will allow other rulers to take His people from their homeland, and Israel will no longer have its own king. Away from their own country, the Israelites won't have the opportunity to practice the ritual sacrifices God had prescribed. Nor will they have access to the high places with sacred pillars that honored false gods. The people might have sometimes used an ephod—part of a priest's clothing—to seek information about the future (see 1 Samuel 23:6–11). Because of this, it had become an idol. The exile would separate them from the ephod and put a stop to this practice. When enemies drove the Israelites from their land, they would not be able to take their household gods with them. Yahweh promises He will orchestrate events so His people will no longer have access to either the false gods of Canaan or the sacred rituals the Israelites had tainted. But He has a purpose for this action:

> Afterward the children of Israel shall return and seek the
> LORD their God, and David their king, and they shall come in
> fear to the LORD and to His goodness in the latter days.
> (Hosea 3:5)

Yahweh hopes that when all distractions are removed, His beloved will return to Him. God wants nothing more than for His people to pursue Him—to seek Him as Lord *and* to seek David their king (a prophecy of the Messiah, descendant of David's royal line). Yahweh longs for the people to come to Him in awe of His goodness.

Yahweh longs for the people to come to Him in awe of His goodness.

GOMER

In reading Hosea 3, my first question isn't "Why did Hosea need to buy back Gomer?" Instead, I wonder, "Why did she leave him in the first place?" After all, why would Gomer run out on a man who promised love and faithfulness, especially if she had been passed around as a human commodity in the past?

Did she leave because she felt too confined living with one man when she had become accustomed to many lovers? Did she miss the fringe benefits—money and jewelry and a fancier lifestyle—that other lovers gave but a humble prophet couldn't afford? Did she abandon Hosea because she had married him only to get out of her horrid situation and didn't actually love him? Or perhaps she returned to her old life because she acutely felt the shame of her past or sensed that everyone in Hosea's circle judged her. Maybe Gomer simply wished to go where she fit in— even if it meant going back to a sad and depressing life.

Perhaps you have had similar feelings at times. Although you've experienced God's goodness, maybe following Him has felt stifling. The world around you offers many seemingly attractive options, and at times you think, *Why should I limit myself?*

Or maybe you follow the Lord because it's the right thing to do. From your time as a child in Sunday School until now, you've been taught to obey the Ten Commandments and go to church—so you do. But would anyone characterize your relationship with God as passionate?

Or perhaps you come from a not-so-stellar past. When you attend church and sit with the people who know the hymns and where to find the Bible passage the pastor is talking about, you feel out of place. Satan pushes the shame button in your heart and tells you that you don't belong. You have a hard time convincing yourself that God and His people could actually accept you. You think, *Maybe I should go back to my old life.*

We don't know why Gomer left Hosea, but we do know that she got herself into some trouble. She needed rescuing. Perhaps when she first abandoned the marriage, she quickly ran out of money and had no means of supporting herself. Maybe she found someone who promised to care for her (in return for certain benefits), but all the while he maintained a running tab of Gomer's expenses.[22] If imprisoned in a cell of debt, she couldn't leave until she paid what she owed.

Thankfully, Hosea obeyed the Lord's instructions and came to Gomer's rescue. How did Gomer feel now? Did gratitude bubble out of her heart for the man who loved her enough to rescue her twice? Did she feel loved and valued when Hosea showed up?

Scripture tells us Hosea bought Gomer for the price of "fifteen shekels of silver and a homer and a lethech of barley" (Hosea 3:2). Just in case you haven't had to convert shekels and homers and lethechs lately, this amounted to about six ounces of silver and nine or ten bushels of barley, altogether about thirty shekels of silver—a significant amount, since this was the value of a human slave (see Exodus 21:32).

HOSEA IN THE NEW TESTAMENT: THIRTY PIECES OF SILVER

The price Hosea paid to redeem Gomer may bring to mind another passage in Scripture that mentions thirty pieces of silver. Judas received that amount for delivering Jesus to the chief priests. The almighty Son of God was sold for the price of a slave.

Jesus willingly took our place as slaves to sin, suffering all the punishment we deserved. Christ acted as the proxy slave and as the Redeemer of all slaves.

Perhaps shame pricked Gomer again when she heard that Hosea had paid the price of a slave to free her. Instead of gratitude, she may have felt humiliation. Hosea had taken her from her miserable life, cared for her, and given her children. She had repaid him by ignoring everything he did for her and leaving him to seek more excitement, only to find herself in an even more deplorable situation. Once in debt, she had no means to free herself. She needed to be rescued again by the man she had deserted. Perhaps she thought, *How can I even look him the eye? How could he ever love me again? How could he treat me as anything but a slave? After all, that's all I'm worth.*

We've all had times in our lives when we've acted somewhat like Gomer. We've ignored God's Word and His reassurances of love and we've gone off looking for something more exciting, more tangible. Along the way, we've become involved with the wrong people and gotten entangled in projects or businesses we know wouldn't meet our Lover's approval. We've hurt people, said things we wish we could take back, and stormed off in a huff. We've lost it when we've argued with our husband, our friends, or that horrible clerk at the big box store. Maybe we've crossed the line sexually, fudged an IRS form, or lied to a boss.

It's then that we wonder, *How could God love me again? Surely He will never take me back into His arms. This time I've gone too far.*

Like Gomer, who needed to be bought for the price of a slave, we can become enslaved by disgrace. Sure of our worthlessness, we may replay shame's accusations: "You will never amount to anything." "You're a lousy mother." "No one could ever love you." So we try to free ourselves from the constant loop of blame playing in our mind by improving ourselves. We read a few self-help books, sign up for some goal-strategizing sessions. We promise ourselves that we won't lose our temper, won't answer the phone call from the person who looks so right but we know is so wrong. But every time we take a step forward, shame snaps the chains and pulls us backward. Shame tells us that we could never deserve God's love.

BROKEN OR NOT SO BAD?

When you first opened the Book of Hosea, you may have immediately identified with Gomer—a broken woman living a broken life. On the other hand, you might have thought, *At least I'm not as bad as that. Someone like Gomer may need rescuing, but I'm doing fine on my own.*

Satan can use both sets of tapes in our minds. At times he will try to keep us enslaved in shame and convince us we can never experience God's love because we don't deserve it. We ignore God's rescuing work and shut out His words of affection because we're certain they aren't meant for us.

At other times, Satan will try to convince us that we don't need God's grace as much as that sinful woman over there. Satan tempts us to think, *She might need saving, but I'm pretty sure I can handle my own problems.* When we snub God's grace because we don't feel a need for it, we will find ourselves bound up in pride.

Let's all watch out for Satan's lies. No one deserves God's mercy, but because of Jesus' redemptive work, He offers it to each of us freely through the Gospel of His glorious grace. He can unlock the chains of shame and the shackles of pride.

HOSEA

We've examined the situation from Gomer's point of view; now let's imagine it from Hosea's. Even though the prophet might not have responded enthusiastically to God's request to find Gomer and bring her back, he obeys.

Up to this point in Hosea's book, we have not had the opportunity to listen in on any of Hosea and Gomer's conversations. Therefore, because the first words spoken by a biblical figure carry special significance,[23] we pay attention when Hosea tells Gomer:

You must dwell as mine for many days. You shall not play the
whore, or belong to another man; so will I also be to you.
(Hosea 3:3)

Hosea gave both tender promises and strict conditions to his wife.

Hosea reassured Gomer of a long-term relationship. He said, "You
must dwell as mine *for many days*" (emphasis added). He would not bring
her back home only to kick her out in a week.

Hosea emphasized her belonging. When he said, "You must dwell
as *mine*" (emphasis added), he stressed the exclusivity of the relationship, but he also spoke of Gomer as a part of his family and household.

Hosea gave Gomer boundaries. He told his wife, "You shall not play
the whore, or belong to another man." A loving marriage is made up of
only two people—all others are excluded. Love often means setting limits.

Hosea promised faithful love. After he asked Gomer for her complete love and undivided attention, he promised the same to her: "So will
I also be to you."

Hosea didn't buy back his wife simply to stop her trade as a prostitute. He redeemed her to bring her back into relationship with him.

YAHWEH

Hosea's words to Gomer summarize the entire message of all fourteen chapters of the book. As Hosea spoke those words to his wife, Yahweh spoke them to Israel, His beloved: "You will be Mine for many days.
But our relationship must be exclusive. You can't give yourself to other
gods, other lovers. I promise My faithfulness to you." And because we are
the Bride of Christ, God speaks these words to us as well.

God reassures us of a long-term relationship. Yahweh told the people of Israel, and us, "I have loved you with an everlasting love; therefore I
have continued My faithfulness to you" (Jeremiah 31:3). Other relationships
may come and go, but God's love endures. Some marriages, like Dick and
Mary's, last sixty-plus years, but our relationship with the Lord lasts forever.

God tells us we belong to Him. Isaiah wrote God's words, "Fear not, for I have redeemed you; I have called you by name, you are Mine" (Isaiah 43:1). We all yearn for belonging. We want to be a part of a family or a supportive group of friends. Most of all, we desire to belong to someone who loves us above all others. Some of you may have experienced this in a loving marriage, but we can all have the exceptional privilege of belonging in Christ.

God gives us boundaries. Satan wants us to believe that God's instructions exist to make us miserable. He tries to convince us that we'll miss out on all the fun if we follow God's Law. But God gave us limits because He knows what will lead to happiness and what will only be a dead end of disappointment and regret. In Psalm 119:45, the psalmist says, "And I shall walk in a wide place, for I have sought out Your precepts." God's precepts (another word for laws) give us freedom to walk in the spacious place of God's love, protected from dangers we can't see.

God's precepts give us freedom to walk in the spacious place of God's love, protected from dangers we can't see.

God promises His faithful love. Romans 8:38–39 says, "For I am sure that neither death nor life, nor angels nor rulers, nor things present nor things to come, nor powers, nor height nor depth, nor anything else in all creation, will be able to separate us from the love of God in Christ Jesus our Lord." What comfort to know that nothing can disconnect us from God's relentless love.

This tenacious love meant God had to pay a price. Just as Hosea paid the equivalent of thirty shekels so Gomer could come back to him, Yahweh redeemed the people of Israel, and Christ redeemed us. Hosea's purchase of his wife foreshadows what Jesus did for all of us. Hosea bought his wife back for the price of a slave, but redeeming us required a much higher price. The apostle Peter writes, "You were ransomed from the futile ways inherited from your forefathers, not with perishable things such as silver or gold, but with the precious blood of Christ, like that of a lamb without blemish or spot" (1 Peter 1:18–19). Christ willingly paid the highest price possible to bring us to Him.

MARRIAGE AND DIVORCE

When you read the story of Hosea, you might wonder if God commands all of us to take back unfaithful spouses. Is that the Christian thing to do?

God created marriage as a lifelong commitment between a man and a woman. Just as Hosea said to Gomer, "You shall not . . . belong to another man; so will I also be to you" (Hosea 3:3), each marriage partner should love the other exclusively for life.

In the New Testament, Jesus said, "Whoever divorces his wife, except for sexual immorality, and marries another, commits adultery" (Matthew 19:9). "God forbids divorce except for marital unfaithfulness (adultery and malicious desertion)."[24] Because of Gomer's adultery and desertion, Hosea had the right to divorce her. However, in this particular case, God asked His prophet to go above and beyond what was required. Yahweh wanted Hosea's actions to portray how He loved Israel more than she deserved.

God's instructions to Hosea do not become requirements for us. We do not have to remain in situations where we experience unfaithfulness or violence. The Bible allows for marriages broken by adultery, abuse, or abandonment to be reconciled, but it doesn't demand it.

LIVE LIKE YOU'RE LOVED

The wonderful message of the third chapter of Hosea is this: God will not abandon you when you're at your lowest point. You may have walked away from Him and given your heart to someone or something else. You may have ignored your most important Lover to seek excitement in another, but Yahweh won't leave you there. He tells you, tells me, "You don't need to wallow in your past, in your mistakes, in your shame."

God will not abandon you when you're at your lowest point.

Of course, Satan wants you to stay mired in your humiliation, guilt, and feelings of worthlessness. He will whisper the lie over and over that God couldn't possibly love a mess like you. Or the myth that you need to get your act together before you can go back to Him. Or the lie that you need to prove your value to be worthy of His love. He repeats versions of these falsehoods over and again so we don't reach out and receive the love and grace God freely gives.

But we find God's truth in the message of an ancient prophet: God's love never gives up on you. His relentless love means He paid the highest price possible to win you back. He paid the price with His own Son's blood. Now God stands with open arms, ready for you to return. He says to each of us, "I'll take you at your worst—when you've rejected My love and sought happiness in other people, other pursuits, other loves. I'll take all your shame, brokenness, and lost hope and transform it into a second honeymoon. You belong to Me."

Remember Dick and Mary's story? Their sixty-eight-year marriage is a beautiful example of lasting love. But God's love for you endures even longer. His affection for you persists even stronger. His faithfulness means He will continually pursue you, seek your attention, and strive to bring you back to Him when you've walked away. Let's all reject Satan's lies and embrace the truth of God's unceasing affection for us. When we step into Christ's relentless and redeeming love, the shackles of guilt and the chains of shame fall to the ground.

CHAPTER FOUR

A RELENTLESS LOVE STORY

"Something seems wrong," the preschool teachers told Scott and Sophie. "We suggest you have Logan evaluated. His physical skills don't meet with what we expect at age 3."

Stunned but not yet alarmed, Scott and Sophie followed up on the suggestion for their son. School district personnel assessed Logan's development, then called Sophie into a meeting where seven people sat across the table from her and said, "We don't know exactly what's wrong, but you need to make an appointment with a doctor." Their trusted pediatrician ran some tests, and five days after Logan's fourth birthday, she gave his parents the news: "The numbers on your son's bloodwork indicate one of two things. Either he has had a heart attack or he has muscular dystrophy." Knowing Logan had not suffered a heart attack, they knew the certainty of the other option. They took it as a death sentence.

The next few months were spent with doctors at the children's hospital in Chicago and specialists from the Muscular Dystrophy Association (MDA) as they learned more about Logan's particular form of the disease—Duchenne muscular dystrophy, a genetic disorder with progressive muscular degeneration and weakness. Doctors gave them the grim news that patients with Duchenne rarely survive past their late teens or early twenties. How could their seemingly healthy four-year-old have this disease?

From then on, Scott and Sophie shuttled Logan to doctors, specialists, physical therapists, and occupational therapists to keep the disease at bay. They did stretching exercises every day at home, yet Logan slowly lost flexibility, strength, and stamina. He began walking more and more pigeon-toed as his leg muscles tightened up. By age 7, he used a wheelchair when he needed to go longer distances.

Then tragedy upon tragedy struck. Sophie received a call from her family in North Dakota that her mother was in the hospital and was experiencing heart problems. Things looked serious, so Sophie jumped into the car and began the long drive from the Chicago area to North Dakota. While driving through Minnesota, Sophie's car was struck in a multivehicle accident. She died moments after first responders arrived. Scott now faced life without his beloved wife and caregiving partner. Even as he began a new grieving process, he faced the arduous task of raising an eleven-year-old boy with muscular dystrophy alone.

Though it was a difficult journey, Scott's relentless love for his son got Logan through middle school, high school, and the continued loss of motor function. Wheelchair-bound since age 12, Logan now attends the University of Illinois at Champaign-Urbana as a creative writing major and lives in a dorm for students with special needs. U of I has a marvelous program that allows twenty-year-old Logan to hire other students, trained by the university, to get him ready in the morning, take him for bathroom breaks, and put him to bed in the evening. He uses a motorized wheelchair and the bus system to get to his classes. This arrangement allows Logan some independence and gives Scott a break.

But when Logan comes home during breaks, Scott again takes care of his son's daily needs, such as getting him out of bed, brushing his teeth, and helping him get dressed. All of this requires the relentless care of a loving father.

Through it all, Logan has had a strong faith. Scott recalls an incident that happened when, at age 8, Logan became the MDA Goodwill Ambassador for the State of Illinois. The whole family attended many fund-raising events where organizers not only interviewed Logan but played a video outlining the grim facts of Duchenne muscular dystrophy—including life expectancy. One day while riding to one of these events, Logan asked his parents, "Am I going to die?"

Sophie explained, "Everybody dies. We don't know where or when. But it's a glorious thing for those who believe in God." Scott says he believes Logan has been able to deal with the losses of his mother and his mobility because of his deep faith in Christ.

I so admire Scott's relentless love for Logan. He tries to play down his role, saying, "As a parent, anyone will do whatever they need to for their child." But Scott faces more difficulties than most of us in the parenting department. He does it without complaining and says, "I don't see Logan as handicapped. I see him as a typical twenty-year-old who likes the Cubs, video games, and hanging with his friends."

God's Relentless Love Restores

Hosea 4–7

MEMORY VERSE

Let us know; let us press on to know the LORD;
His going out is sure as the dawn;
He will come to us as the showers,
as the spring rains that water the earth.

Hosea 6:3

When have you experienced the relentless love of someone who cared for you when you felt weak or helpless? Perhaps you went through a time when you needed extra medical care and your spouse gently nursed you back to health without grumbling. Or maybe depression and despair settled in your soul for a season, and you had friends who stood by you even when you had trouble simply leaving the house.

In Hosea, we see the God who relentlessly loves us, even when our own strength fails us. In fact, our heavenly Father longs for us to come to Him when we struggle, when life seems overwhelming, when we find ourselves in impossible situations. However, instead of going to God, we often seek help from rocky road ice cream, retail therapy, or Hallmark movies—and our relationship with God suffers. Yet, no matter how far we've strayed, God continually invites us to return so He can restore our bond with Him.

Let's review what we've learned so far in Hosea. In the first chapter, God instructed the prophet to marry Gomer, an unfaithful woman, as a living picture of God's relentless love for Israel. The couple had three children and God assigned them names that foretold what would happen to two-timing Israel. The second chapter shows how the Lord courted Israel in two ways—bringing charges of unfaithfulness against her, yet pursuing her in an effort to draw her back to Him. In chapter 3, Hosea bought back his own adulterous wife—a parallel to Christ's redeeming love for us, His Bride, the Church.

The Hosea-Gomer love story provides a picture of the relationship of Yahweh with His people, Israel, and a metaphor for our relationship with a God who relentlessly loves. Throughout the rest of the book, however, Hosea never mentions Gomer. Chapters 4–14 of Hosea record the messages the prophet delivered to Israel in an effort to bring the people back into relationship with the one true God. We see echoes of Hosea's life picture, but he does not specifically mention his marriage.

MORE CHARGES AGAINST ISRAEL

At the end of Hosea 2, we thought court had adjourned, but in chapter 4, the Lord reconvenes court and brings more charges against Israel.

> Hear the word of the LORD, O children of Israel,
> for the LORD has a controversy with the inhabitants of
> the land.
> There is no faithfulness or steadfast love,
> and no knowledge of God in the land. (Hosea 4:1)

God lists three sins of omission: no faithfulness, no steadfast love, no knowledge of God. The people continually act unfaithfully; they are about as trustworthy as a puppy with your bacon sandwich. Their love is not the kind of love God wants. *Hesed*, the Hebrew word for "love" here, describes a love characterized by devotion. The people think they know God, but knowledge of God means much more than knowing facts about Him. The knowledge God desires implies knowing someone intimately and personally. Like unfaithful Gomer, Israel abandoned its covenant relationship with Yahweh. It seems they don't even know Him anymore.

The knowledge God desires implies knowing someone intimately and personally.

Next, God charges the people with sins of commission:

> There is swearing, lying, murder, stealing, and committing
>   adultery;
> they break all bounds, and bloodshed follows bloodshed.
> (Hosea 4:2)

Swearing, lying, murder, stealing, committing adultery—all five of these sins go against the Ten Commandments, God's Law for His covenant people. Yahweh gives evidence of these sins: The men go to harlots and sacrifice with cult prostitutes (see v. 14). It's almost unthinkable, but fathers took their daughters to the cult shrines to serve sexually (see v. 13). The state of the nation had sunk so low that the priests became "greedy for their iniquity" (v. 8); the more the people sinned, the more sin offerings they brought, and the more the priests benefited personally from these sacrifices. God says even the "rulers dearly love shame" (v. 18).

In Hosea 5, Yahweh continues His charges against His people and announces His judgment. Perhaps because they experienced economic prosperity during the years of Jeroboam II, they thought they could get away with their infidelity. But God tells them He has seen their unfaithfulness: "I know Ephraim, and Israel is not hidden from Me; for now, O Ephraim, you have played the whore; Israel is defiled" (Hosea 5:3). God has words for the southern nation as well: "The pride of Israel testifies to his face; Israel and Ephraim shall stumble in his guilt; Judah also shall stumble with them" (v. 5).

In the middle of the charges, Hosea the prophet breaks in with a call to the people to return to the Lord (Hosea 6:1–3). But God sees their unreliable ways and their insincere repentance. Like a frustrated parent, the Lord says:

> What shall I do with you, O Ephraim?
> What shall I do with you, O Judah?

Your love is like a morning cloud,

    like the dew that goes early away. (Hosea 6:4)

Perhaps the people professed a love for God, but it disappeared as quickly as an early morning fog or dew on the grass.

Chapter 7 continues with evidence of Israel's sins: "They deal falsely; the thief breaks in, and the bandits raid outside" (v. 1). God compares their adultery to a heated oven (see v. 4): "The hearts of the Israelite people and princes are hot with lust for idol worship and wickedness, hot as a baker's fire that needs no stirring up the whole time he is mixing and kneading the bread."[25]

A CAKE NOT TURNED

In Hosea 7:8, God describes Ephraim (the nation Israel) as "a cake not turned." In Bible times, ovens were cylindrical, domed structures with a large door on top. The baker would build a blazing fire inside the structure and, when only glowing coals remained, press round, flat loaves against the interior clay walls.[26]

Some scholars think "a cake not turned" describes pancake-shaped bread that a cook had not turned over, leaving the cake burned on one side and undercooked on the other. Someone looking into the oven might not have seen the damage. If Hosea meant this type of cake, the word picture informed the people that although their nation might *appear* prosperous, God could see their ruined hearts.[27]

Other scholars point out that no evidence exists to show that bakers turned the cakes in the clay ovens. They think "a cake not turned" refers to a loaf that was not doubled over before baking and was therefore insubstantial and flimsy. Either analogy pictures Ephraim as weak and of poor quality.[28]

THEY RETURN, BUT NOT UPWARD

In this section of the book, God repeatedly charges Israel with the crime of turning to other nations for help. Instead of crying out to the covenant God of love, they sought help from worldly sources. Like Gomer, who left Hosea for the love and nurture of other men, Israel rejected God's care and turned to others for strength and protection:

> When Ephraim saw his sickness,
>   and Judah his wound,
> then Ephraim went to Assyria,
>   and sent to the great king.
> But he is not able to cure you
>   or heal your wound. (Hosea 5:13)

Ephraim and Judah recognize their disease, but they go to the wrong source for healing. Israel acts like a bird flitting foolishly back and forth:

> Ephraim is like a dove,
>   silly and without sense,
>   calling to Egypt, going to Assyria. (Hosea 7:11)

While Hosea likely wrote the opening chapters of his book during the reign of Jeroboam II, scholars think he penned the words of chapter 7 during the Syro-Ephraimite War (736–732 BC) involving Israel's King Pekah, Syria's King Rezin, and Judah's King Jotham.[29] Hosea's ministry lasted many years and outlasted many kings.

KINGS DURING HOSEA'S DAY

Hosea opens his book with a reference to the years he served God as prophet: "The word of the LORD that came to Hosea, the son of Beeri, in the days of Uzziah, Jotham, Ahaz, and Hezekiah, kings of Judah, and in the days of Jeroboam the son of Joash, king of Israel" (Hosea 1:1). Even though he ministered mainly to the Northern Kingdom, he listed only one king of Israel and four kings of Judah. Through the historical books of 1 and 2 Kings, we can determine the kings who reigned in Israel at the same time. The following table gives historical background of this turbulent time for these nations.[30]

KINGS OF JUDAH	KINGS OF ISRAEL (EPHRAIM)
Uzziah (792–740)	Jeroboam II (793–753)
Jotham (750–735)	Zechariah (753; reigned 6 months)
	Shallum (752; reigned 1 month) Menahem (752–742)
Ahaz (735–715)	Pekahiah (742–740) Pekah (740–732)
	Hoshea (732–722)

As you can see from the chart, royalty in Israel had a high turnover rate. And if you read 2 Kings 14–17, you will discover that many changes in reign happened via assassination. If life insurance had existed in the eighth century BC, Israelite kings would have had very high premiums!

The historical record in 2 Kings also shows how some of the rulers sought help from the world powers of their day to retain their rule.

Menahem. According to 2 Kings 15:19, in order "to confirm his hold on the royal power," King Menahem gave the king of Assyria (modern-day Iraq) a thousand talents of silver—about thirty-seven tons![31]

Pekah. When King Tiglath-pileser of Assyria captured many cities of Israel during King Pekah's rule, Pekah joined forces with Rezin, king of Aram (also known as Syria), to attempt to defeat King Ahaz of Judah and set up a king of their own choosing to have another ally against Assyria.

Ahaz. The prophet Isaiah warned King Ahaz of the plans of Pekah and Rezin and urged Ahaz to turn to God for protection (see Isaiah 7:7–9). Instead, godless Ahaz gave all the silver and gold from the temple to Tiglath-pileser to obtain his help (see 2 Kings 16:7–8).

Hoshea. Not to be confused with the prophet Hosea, King Hoshea essentially acted as a puppet king controlled by Assyria, retaining his rule because of the tribute he paid to Tiglath-pileser. When Tiglath-pileser's son took over as king, Hoshea tried to get out of the arrangement by seeking help from Egypt—help that never came.[32]

In the end, Assyria invaded Israel and laid siege to the capital city of Samaria for three years (see 2 Kings 17:5). Assyrian clay tablets record the words of the Assyrian king who achieved the victory in 722 BC: "I (Sargon) besieged and conquered Samaria, led away as booty 27,290 inhabitants."[33] Hoshea was the last king of Israel. Judah continued as a nation for another century but eventually fell in 587 BC.

The people of Israel and Judah had good reason to fear the Assyrians, who were infamous for their brutal style of warfare. They had massive, trained armies and great siege machines operated by engineers. The Assyrians also employed psychological warfare by impaling corpses on stakes and constructing piles of severed heads.[34]

But even if they knew all about the terror of Assyria, the people of Israel and Judah should not have feared that nation or any other foreign power. They should have recalled that they could rely on the God who rescued them from Egypt—the greatest world power at that time. They should have remembered that they could turn to the God who defeated Goliath and other Philistine giants.

Yet the people ignored God's desire to come to their aid. God sent prophets like Hosea, Isaiah, Joel, and Amos to call the people to repentance and draw them back to the God who persistently loved them, yet the people continued their unfaithful ways. God said of their two-timing habits, "They return, but not upward" (Hosea 7:16). Like a mixed-up middle-schooler who shuns the help of a kind teacher and turns to the resident mean girl for backup, the Israelites didn't turn their gaze upward to the Lord but instead, they turned to other nations for help—nations that would later defeat and mock them.

WE RETURN, BUT NOT UPWARD

Looking at the sad history of Israel and Judah, we might wonder how they could have gone so wrong. After witnessing the power of an almighty God, how could they have turned to world powers—scary as they might be—for help?

Yet, how often we do the same thing! When seemingly impossible situations invade our lives, we might think, *This situation is too big, too challenging for God to work.* We forget the mind-blowing power of the

God who created the universe, split the Red Sea, and raised His Son from the tomb. Instead, we panic and turn to the internet for advice and to the money in our bank accounts for security.

Even when not facing a crisis, I may find myself turning to worldly sources for guidance and acceptance instead of to my omnipotent Father. My position at my workplace may determine my self-worth more than my position in the kingdom of God. It may seem more concrete to seek guidance from life coaches and financial advisors than to send up a prayer to a God I can't see. But although I sometimes need the wisdom of doctors, advisors, and counselors, I always need to remember that God's power to change my life dwarfs worldly sources of help.

The invincible God who relentlessly loves reminds us that we don't have to continue to try harder in our own strength. He *wants* to help us. He *longs* for us to "turn upward."

The invincible God who relentlessly loves reminds us that we don't have to continue to try harder in our own strength. He *wants* to help us.

I've been guilty of turning any direction but upward when looking for guidance and support. A few years ago, after writing a couple of books, I wanted to expand my reach as an author. I discovered a program that promised to get me more readers. Lured by the assurance that if I followed the program, I could become a major influencer, I signed up. Every week, I listened to expert after expert share their formulas for successful blogging practices and social media routines. But although I faithfully attempted every strategy, I never attained the results promised by that sea of experts. Looking back, I see I acted just like the Israelites who went to worldly powers instead of Yahweh for help. I relied on social media and tech experts for guidance instead of my omnipotent, omniscient God.

I had a lot in common with the Israelites. We both desired big, important positions in our world. We both relied on human sources for strength instead of turning to God. And in both cases, Yahweh allowed all those human-based efforts to fail so we would return to Him, repent of our pride, and ask for His wisdom and aid.

As humans, we dislike admitting our weaknesses. Remember the story of Scott and his son, Logan, who struggles with muscular dystrophy? Spiritually, we all have muscular dystrophy. In fact, we have no ability to save ourselves, and yet we try to deny that truth. Perhaps we even put on a mask of strength and confidence because we wonder if God could love someone feeble and needy. But just as Scott doesn't love Logan any less because he can no longer walk, God loves us no less in our weakness. Instead of looking down on us because of our frailty and flaws, He invites us to use our failings as an opportunity to witness His ability to restore our broken lives.

Instead of looking down on us because of our frailty and flaws, God invites us to use our failings as an opportunity to witness His ability to restore our broken lives.

What struggles do you face? In what areas does life seem like greater effort with fewer results? Perhaps, like me, you have turned to worldly sources of strength instead of to your loving God. In his commentary on Hosea, Paul E. Eickmann writes:

> If we are accomplishing less and less in the Lord's service, we easily turn to other helpers. Instead, we need to examine our relationship to him. Does he own our hearts, or have we given them to other gods? Are we depending on the power of the Lord as his Spirit works through Word and sacraments?[35]

THE THIRD DAY

In Hosea 6:2, the prophet writes, "After two days He will revive us; on the third day He will raise us up, that we may live before Him." The references to "two days" and "the third day" tell the people that restoration won't happen immediately but sometime in the future. These words also remind us how God acted on the third day after Christ's crucifixion, raising Him from the dead. Jesus' triumph over death and Satan heals our sin-sick hearts and restores our wounded relationship with God. What a glorious truth!

PRESS ON TO KNOW THE LORD

I don't know about you, but I tend to turn to human sources of strength when I forget who God is. Throughout Hosea 4–7, the prophet charges the people with ignorance of God. In effect, he told them, "I don't see any knowledge of God in the land" (see 4:1). "You've rejected knowledge, and that lack of knowledge will be your undoing" (see 4:6). "Yahweh laments the fact that you—His own people—don't know Him, though you claim to seek Him with your hypocritical sacrifices" (see 5:6–7).

So the prophet calls out to his neighbors:

> Come, let us return to the LORD;
>   for He has torn us, that He may heal us;
>   He has struck us down, and He will bind us up.
> After two days He will revive us;
>   on the third day He will raise us up,
>   that we may live before Him.
> Let us know; let us press on to know the LORD;
>   His going out is sure as the dawn;
> He will come to us as the showers,
>   as the spring rains that water the earth. (Hosea 6:1–3)

Can you hear the urgency in Hosea's plea? He appeals to his contemporaries and to us, "Let's pursue a deeper knowledge of God, because the better we know Him, the more we will recognize His constancy. He's as faithful as the daily event of the sun rising. He's as reliable as the yearly occurrence of spring rains. He continuously brings light to our dark souls and refreshment to our weary hearts—if we turn to Him."

Unfortunately, the people of Hosea's day didn't turn to God. And because of their disobedience and neglect of their sacred relationship with Yahweh, He eventually tore them from their homeland. But He did this for a purpose: God tore only so He could heal. He struck down so the people would return, and He could be the one to bind their wounds.

Let's pursue a deeper relationship with the almighty Lord, who holds us close through every hardship, every heartache.

Let's not act like the people of Israel, who ignored God's call to return to Him. Let's not behave like Gomer, who left a loving husband and turned to other men to meet her needs. Instead, may we remember that the One who calls us "beloved" longs to come to our aid whenever trouble pushes its way into our lives. Let's pursue a deeper relationship with the almighty Lord, who holds us close through every hardship, every heartache.

HOSEA IN THE NEW TESTAMENT

Jesus quoted Hosea 6:6 when He told the Pharisees, "Go and learn what this means: 'I desire mercy, and not sacrifice'" (Matthew 9:13). Hosea originally spoke those words to the Israelites, who thought they could please God with outward sacrifices, without the inward devotion of their hearts. Jesus used Hosea's words to confront the Pharisees, who also emphasized outward rituals and rules. Jesus' words remind us all that what God truly desires is our hearts.

LIVE LIKE YOU'RE LOVED

Not only does Hosea invite all of us to "press on to know the LORD" (Hosea 6:3), God Himself tells us how much He desires us to know Him. He says:

> For I desire steadfast love and not sacrifice,
> the *knowledge* of God rather than burnt offerings.
> (Hosea 6:6, emphasis added)

The Hebrew word for "knowledge," *da`ath*, and its root word, *yada*, mean much more than knowing interesting facts about someone. These words describe a knowledge that is not only based on observation but also grounded in experience.[36] In Genesis, the word *yada* describes the most intimate relationship of a husband with his wife (see Genesis 4:1). Pastor Geoffrey Boyle writes, "Knowledge here is a relationship, a union, an intimate bond. This knowledge pertains not just to the head but also the heart and the soul. What Israel lacks is the intimate relationship with the Lord: the fear, trust, and love in God above all things."[37]

Let's not settle for a superficial relationship with Christ. Ask yourself, "Does my relationship with God look more like a marriage or like a Facebook friendship?" On social media, I can learn that a certain friend lives in Kansas, teaches at an elementary school, and likes musicals, even though I've never met her. But I know much more about my husband. Besides knowing where he lives and works, I know the tough time he had growing up with an alcoholic father. I know his gifts for woodworking and making me laugh. I know his heart for visiting hurting people.

Let's not settle for a superficial relationship with Christ.

How amazing that the God who created the universe wants you to know Him as intimately as you know your spouse or best friend! That the God who formed galaxies and planets wants you to become better acquainted with Him. That the God who keeps the world spinning on its axis hopes you will come close enough to know He loves you despite your flaws and failures. That the One who composed the songs of birds and the babble of brooks aches for you to know more of His power to defeat all your fear, soothe all your pain, and restore all your brokenness.

So live like you're loved. Spend time with God, who wants to draw you close. Open His love letter to you, and hear Him call you "chosen," "beloved," "cherished." Have deep conversations with the One who longs to hear your sorrows and disappointments, your hopes and dreams. Sit in His presence so He can heal your hurts and restore your soul. Receive His gifts in the Holy Meal He prepares just for you. Press on to know the God who relentlessly loves.

CHAPTER FIVE

A Relentless Love Story

"Shelly, you don't know how to choose men," a friend told my sister. "Let me pick one out for you."

Coming out of a bad marriage, Shelly didn't want to jump into another relationship. But her friend insisted that guys didn't come any better than David, a mutual acquaintance who was the construction manager of Shelly's subdivision, so she agreed to have dinner with him. On the evening of the date, David picked Shelly up and began driving to the restaurant. But as he drove along back streets she didn't recognize, Shelly thought, *I have no idea where we are! What is this guy up to? I should have said I would meet him at the restaurant.*

Eventually, they arrived at their destination. Shelly was enjoying her meal until the server came by and took David's empty plate. "She's done with hers too," David told the server. Shelly watched her still-half-full plate disappear from the table before she could protest that she still wanted her food!

After that first date, Shelly was hesitant to agree to a second, but David made every effort to connect with her. Because his work meant he would be supervising projects in Shelly's subdivision, he made a point to learn about her work schedule. David began timing his arrival to the neighborhood with her departure for work. When he saw her car approach, he would wave for her to slow down. She would stop her car and roll down her window for a minute of small talk before continuing her drive to work. David relentlessly pursued these daily conversations.

Shelly didn't want to tell her young son, Seth, about David right away, in case the relationship went nowhere. So, she scheduled her dates with David for evenings when Seth stayed with his father. However, Seth was acquainted with David because of his work in the neighborhood. In fact, fun-loving David often got the boys of the subdivision together to play ball. Unaware of the developing situation, Seth told his mother, "If you ever want to start dating, you should date David."

After months of clandestine meetings, Shelly told Seth about the relationship, and the three of them began spending time together. David earned a lot of points when Shelly saw that he cared about Seth and had a positive influence on him. Still, she hesitated about a long-term involvement, but David kept trying. He even appealed to her accounting persona: "Just think of the deductions we'll have at tax time if we get married!"

One day when she arrived home from work and saw David standing in the garage with Seth, she finally made up her mind to take the risk. He had come over to cook dinner for the three of them. When she opened her car door, David started smiling and clapping. Looking at Seth and then at Shelly, he shouted, "Mommy's home!" Shelly decided she wouldn't mind having David's enthusiastic love all the time.

David's relentless pursuit of Shelly paid off. She once told me, "David's like a fungus. He grew on me."

God's Relentless Love Rains Righteousness

Hosea 8–10

MEMORY VERSE

Sow for yourselves righteousness;
reap steadfast love;
break up your fallow ground,
for it is the time to seek the LORD,
that He may come and rain righteousness upon you.

Hosea 10:12

My sister's friend cared enough about her to point out her poor choices in men: "Shelly, you don't know how to choose men."

Hosea attempted to share a similar message with the people of Israel: "You don't know how to choose who to worship. Time after time, you give your heart away to the wrong gods. You run to deceptive loves—even when the one true God stands with arms open wide, ready to love you, forgive you, and rescue you."

Honestly, I've also made mistakes in choosing whom and what to love. I've offered my heart to the imitation gods of success, security, and accomplishment. I've attempted to find my worth in anything but God. I've bowed down to the idol of peer approval and worshiped at the altar of busyness.

In Hosea 8–10, the prophet continues to call out to the Israelites, pleading with them to return to the God who relentlessly loves them. God also speaks, pointing out how far His people have strayed from His love. Instead of worshiping Him, they bowed to counterfeit gods made of silver and gold, wood and stone. Though at first glance we might not identify with these idol worshipers, closer examination demonstrates that our lives often parallel theirs when it comes to venerating false gods. And just as God offered forgiveness and righteousness to His rebellious nation, He offers it to our wayward souls.

ISRAEL SENTENCED

In Hosea 8–10, Yahweh begins to conclude the trial against His beloved nation. He starts by listing additional charges and goes on to deliver the sentence their crimes have deserved. Chapter 8 opens with God again lamenting that His beloved people no longer know Him. They cry out, "My God, we—Israel—know You" (v. 2), but Yahweh sees through their empty words. Although they claim knowledge of Yahweh, they continually "spurned the good" (v. 3) and turned away from God's love—all the while seeking other lovers.

God lists their sins:

- They made their own kings by rejecting God's chosen rulers—the descendants of David—and installed their own (v. 4).

- They bowed to idols made by their own hands (v. 4).

- Instead of relying on almighty God, they turned to foreign nations for strength and protection (v. 9).

- Their altars were places of cultic prostitution and sometimes child sacrifice—serious sins against the true God (v. 11).

- They ignored Yahweh's laws for so long that they now considered them strange (v. 12).

Now Yahweh delivers the bad news of their punishment: "For they sow the wind, and they shall reap the whirlwind" (8:7). Their fruitless worship of false gods resembled the scattering of useless seed. Nothing can grow from a breeze, a gust, or even a gale-force hurricane. Therefore, they would reap the whirlwind. The worldly forces Israel relied on would soon turn on them. Assyria would arrive like an F-5 tornado, destroying everything in its path.

Hosea and Yahweh continue to speak words of judgment in chapter 9:

> They shall not remain in the land of the LORD,
>> But Ephraim shall return to Egypt,
>> And they shall eat unclean food in Assyria. (Hosea 9:3)

The people of Israel will experience exile. The phrase "they shall eat unclean food in Assyria" warns them that their future lies in that foreign nation where they will not be able to participate in the firstfruit sacrifices that consecrated their harvest. The Promised Land will become a wasteland; "thorns shall be in their tents" (v. 6). Ironically, Ephraim, which means "doubly fruitful," will bear no fruit at all. Its "root is dried up" (v. 16).[38]

The lack of fruitfulness applies to their offspring as well. God says, "No birth, no pregnancy, no conception!" (v. 11) and "Even though they give birth, I will put their beloved children to death" (v. 16). Perhaps the people will finally see the irony and futility of their worship of Baal, the pagan god of fertility.

Realizing the horror of the message, Hosea pleads with God:

> Give them, O LORD—
>> what will You give?
> Give them a miscarrying womb
>> and dry breasts. (Hosea 9:14)

To spare the people from the gruesomeness of seeing their children slaughtered, the prophet asks God to give no children at all.[39]

While Hosea 8 and 9 listed the charges against Israel and explained the coming punishment, chapter 10 begins by describing Israel in agricultural terms:

> Israel is a luxuriant vine
>> that yields its fruit.
> The more his fruit increased,
>> the more altars he built;
> as his country improved,
>> he improved his pillars. (Hosea 10:1)

PLACES IN HOSEA

Perhaps while you have read Hosea's writings, you have scratched your head and wondered about the locations he mentions. The people of his day would have recognized these places and their historical significance (see the map on page 15). But we need a little explanation.

Egypt and Memphis. The Egyptians enslaved the Israelites for four hundred years. The mention of this country and one of its cities symbolized captivity.

Gibeah. A sickening incident happened in this city during the days of the judges. Sodomites of Gibeah in Benjamin wanted to sexually abuse a visiting Levite but were prevented, so instead, they abused his concubine all night until she died (see Judges 19:22–29). The Levite cut up the body into twelve pieces and sent the pieces to the other eleven tribes of Israel, demanding retribution for the crime. The Benjamites refused to deliver the criminals for punishment, so the rest of the nation went to war against them. Twenty-five thousand Benjamites were killed.[40] Hosea says the people of his day "have deeply corrupted themselves as in the days of Gibeah" (Hosea 9:9).

Baal-peor. Peor refers to a mountain in the neighboring country of Moab.[41] The Israelites passed by this mountain on their way to the Promised Land. The Moabites invited the people of Israel to worship Baal with sexual rites performed with the Moabite women. Sadly, the people succumbed to the temptation and began a long history of sexual sin and worship of false gods (see Numbers 25:1–3).

Gilgal. Located right across the Jordan River from Baal-peor, Gilgal demonstrated Israel's unfaithfulness in two ways. As the site of King Saul's coronation, it represented the beginning of Israel's rejection of God as King. And as a cult center from the days of Joshua through Hosea's time, it characterized the nation's rejection of Yahweh as their one true God.[42]

Under the rule of Jeroboam II, the nation had prospered and expanded. But prosperity caused them to forget God. Instead of thanking Yahweh for their blessings, they turned to other gods. Now God must "break down their altars and destroy their pillars" (v. 2). While the people rejoiced over false gods represented by stone pillars and golden calves, soon they will mourn their loss (see v. 5).

God will send all the nations against His people (see v. 10) and war will begin (see v. 14). Even "the king of Israel shall be utterly cut off" (v. 15). Why does God allow these disasters? Out of love for His people. He disciplines them so their false gods will be destroyed and the help from outside sources will be proven useless. Then His beloved people will seek Him again and He will rain righteousness on them (see v. 12).

HOSEA IN THE NEW TESTAMENT

Hosea prophesied that the Israelites would ask for death rather than endure exile in Assyria. He said, "They shall say to the mountains, 'Cover us,' and to the hills, 'Fall on us'" (Hosea 10:8). Jesus quoted this verse to the women who followed Him through the streets of Jerusalem on the way to the cross:

But turning to them Jesus said, "Daughters of Jerusalem, do not weep for Me, but weep for yourselves and for your children. For behold, the days are coming when they will say, 'Blessed are the barren and the wombs that never bore and the breasts that never nursed!' Then they will begin to say to the mountains, 'Fall on us,' and to the hills, 'Cover us.' For if they do these things when the wood is green, what will happen when it is dry?" (Luke 23:28–31)

Jesus tells the women not to weep for Him because worse events are coming. Then the people will also ask for death rather than torture. If men treat Him—an innocent man—this way, what will they do to a rebellious city full of sinners?[43]

Modern Idols

Like Gomer, who left Hosea for the love of other men, the Israelites continually sought other lovers in the form of counterfeit gods. They ignored the God who relentlessly loved them, and they continued to choose the wrong lovers—lovers that would only let them down.

In Hosea 8–10, God highlighted the idols Israel had crafted, the altars where they had worshiped, and the sacrifices they had made to imitation gods. He warned that they would bear the punishment for their unfaithfulness:

> With their silver and gold they made idols
> for their own destruction. (Hosea 8:4b)

You might think this whole discussion of idols doesn't apply to you. I can hear you saying, "But I don't have a golden statuette standing in my living room. I don't bow down to a silver figurine." Sorry to break the bad news, but a false god doesn't have to look like a carving of a guy with a big belly or an image of a woman with enough arms to imitate an octopus. An idol is anything that captures our hearts, anything that becomes more important than God.

An idol is anything that captures our hearts, anything that becomes more important than God.

In Exodus, Yahweh declares His number one commandment:

> You shall have no other gods before Me. (Exodus 20:3)

Martin Luther explained how gods do not have to look like a bronze statue or carved figure:

> A god means that from which we are to expect all good and in which we are to take refuge in all distress. . . . I say that whatever you set your heart on and put your trust in is truly your God.[44]

The Israelites turned to Baal and Asheroth instead of Yahweh to meet their needs. They bowed down to golden calves and worshiped at high places, thinking those actions would provide fertility and prosperity. Although we don't worship Baal or bow to sacred pillars, to what or to whom do we turn in tough times? What do we cling to and trust in to give us comfort, worth, or significance? Let's use the 2,800-year-old words of a God-seeking prophet to help us recognize modern-day idols.

Shiny gods. Hosea says, "With their silver and gold they made idols" (8:4). While we don't melt our gold to fashion it into figures to worship, we may worship the actual silver and gold—money. We're tempted to rely on it for security. We stockpile it to feel important and safe.

We may not make golden statues, but we may use money to make other idols. Our silver and gold may enable us to make gods of extravagant homes or endless entertainment. We may use it to worship the gods of social standing, peer approval, or even advanced degrees. Although innocent in themselves, these things can become false gods when we pursue them more than the God of unfailing love.

Man-made gods. Yahweh laughs at the gods the Israelites made: "For it is from Israel; a craftsman made it; it is not God" (Hosea 8:6). The prophet Isaiah also mocked the practice of worshiping man-made idols. He described how a man uses half of a cedar tree to build a fire to cook his food and then uses the other half to carve a god to bow down to (Isaiah 44:15). Isaiah shook his head at this madness. "They know not, nor do they discern" (v. 18).

While we may not use knives or chisels to craft statues, our modern culture often worships the man-made gods of success, career, and achievement. Man-made gods can also come in the form of perfectionism, an obsession with fitness, or even an overwhelming desire to have a prominent Christian ministry.

Man-made gods can also come in the form of perfectionism, an obsession with fitness, or even an overwhelming desire to have a prominent Christian ministry.

A man-made god may even look like a pantry that *must* stay organized, a car that *no one* can get dirty, or a to-do list that *always* needs to be completed. Sometimes I am tempted to bow at the altar of accomplishment. My daily to-do list can become an idol when completing every task takes priority over time with God or caring for the people in my life. When my husband asks for help with something, do I take time to help him, even if it means I won't finish my tasks today? When a friend calls with a heartrending problem, do I drop what I'm doing to listen, or do I glance at my to-do list and say I can't talk right now?

Sexual gods. Hosea chides Israel for their lack of faithfulness to God and immoral worship practices: "For you have played the whore, forsaking your God. You have loved a prostitute's wages on all threshing floors" (9:1). Ancient people used threshing floors to sort the useful grain from the useless chaff. At harvest time, threshing floors also became places for religious ceremonies to thank Baal for a successful harvest. These celebrations often included ritual prostitution.[45] Our culture may not use ceremonial prostitution, but it certainly worships sex. Today's world no longer values sex as a gift of marriage but places it on the pedestal of personal rights and preferences.

Hosea's unifying theme of relationship with God reminds us that relationships themselves can become counterfeit gods. Our culture fashions romantic love into a modern idol, implying that happiness cannot exist without it. Even the good relationships of family and friends can become false gods if we trust in them rather than God for security and joy.

RECOGNIZE. REPENT. RECEIVE.

So what are we to do? Let's use three steps to eliminate the counterfeit gods in our lives: Recognize. Repent. Receive.

Recognize. Prayerfully ask God to reveal any idols taking up space on the altar of your heart.

Perhaps you have already identified some potential counterfeit gods as you read about modern-day idols. God desires to be the only God in our lives, the only occupant on the throne of our hearts. But just like Gomer went to other men and the Israelites worshiped other gods, our human hearts have the tendency to cling to bright, shiny objects, personal trophies, and lovers that are no good for us. Luther wrote, "Ask and examine your heart diligently [2 Corinthians 13:5], and you will find out whether it clings to God alone or not."[46]

To examine your heart, consider these questions inspired by the activities of the ancient Israelites:

- "With their silver and gold they made idols" (Hosea 8:4). Look at your checkbook and credit card statements. Where does most of your money go? What do you make financial sacrifices for?

- "A craftsman made it; it is not God" (v. 6). What do you trust for security and validation—your own efforts or God? Has the pursuit of a promotion or obsession with fitness become an idol?

- "Because Ephraim has multiplied altars for sinning, they have become to him altars for sinning" (v. 11). Ephraim (Israel) set up more and more altars to multiple gods. Even though you profess trust in God, do you see where you may have set up altars to modern idols—social media, food, productivity, sports?

- "As for My sacrificial offerings, they sacrifice meat and eat it" (v. 13). What do you make sacrifices for? While we don't burn sacrifices on altars or participate in the abhorrent practice of child sacrifice, do we sometimes sacrifice our family's welfare in the worship of the god of success? Or do we push our children too hard in the worship of our own goals, our own social standing?

- "You have played the whore, forsaking your God" (9:1). The Israelites gave their affection to false gods. Thinking about your last week, who or what got most of your attention or affection?

- "They came to Baal-peor and consecrated themselves to the thing of shame" (v. 10). What do you dedicate yourself to? The Israelites dedicated themselves to Baal and other shameful idols. Today, our favorite sports teams, entertainers, or pastimes may gain more devotion than the Lord. And even good things like social justice, ecological causes, and higher education can become idols if our dedication to them outweighs our commitment to God.

- "Israel . . . improved his pillars" (10:1). What do you constantly strive to enhance and improve? Your relationship with God? Your home? Your social media status? Your appearance? Your career?

- "The inhabitants of Samaria tremble for the calf of Beth-aven. Its people mourn for it . . . for it has departed from them" (v. 5). What would you mourn if you lost it? What might send you into depression if that person, possession, ability, or position disappeared?

The question "What would you mourn for?" points out one of my potential idols. Nine years ago, when my daughter and her family moved to China, I spiraled into a depression because people I loved now lived half a world away. I spent months mourning the loss of physical proximity to these precious family members. Although God gives the good gift of family, even that can't become our main source of contentment. My repeated refusal to accept my situation told God, "You are not enough." When I felt I needed my family more than I needed God, I exhibited a tendency to turn this blessing into an idol of the heart.

Repent. Admit your sin and ask God to remove this idol.

The Israelites refused to give up their syncretistic practices and multiple gods. Although God had chosen them as His very own, they rejected Him as their one and only and searched for other loves. They didn't trust God to meet their needs and went to counterfeit gods for food and protection. Because they wouldn't listen to His prophets and repent of their ways, God declared He would destroy their false gods and carry them away to Assyria (see Hosea 10:6).

THE SHRINES OF BETHEL AND DAN

The first ruler of the Northern Kingdom, Jeroboam I, installed shrines at the cities of Bethel and Dan. He set up two golden calves and said to the people, "You have gone up to Jerusalem long enough. Behold your gods, O Israel, who brought you up out of the land of Egypt" (1 Kings 12:28).

In 1966, excavations at Dan (now Tell el-Qadi) revealed a sacred site that is almost certainly the high place set up by King Jeroboam I in the tenth century BC. During a recent trip to Israel, I was able to visit the very site where the Israelites began their love affair with idols. I saw the shrine's massive stone stairway that led to a masonry platform nearly ten feet high. The golden calf would have stood on this platform. The site also includes a model of a large, four-horned altar, which would have been used for incense and burnt offerings.[47]

Tiglath-pileser, king of Assyria, conquered Dan in 733 BC and probably destroyed the idols located there by the time Hosea wrote about the calf at Beth-aven in Hosea 10:5.[48] Because Bethel had become a cult center in Hosea's day, the prophet used the derogatory name Beth-aven ("house of wickedness") instead of the usual name, Bethel ("house of God").[49]

Instead of clinging to our shiny idols or man-made gods, let's repent of our false worship. Back when my daughter first moved to China, it took months before I recognized that my desire to have my family close by had become an idol. When I finally listened to the Holy Spirit's nudging, I gave God my muddled emotions and confessed my distrust that He alone could meet my needs. I asked the Holy Spirit to help me turn from my obsession and focus on His presence and good gifts to me. And when my heart returned to this idol, I did it again. And again.

Our counterfeit gods aren't always apparent, and admitting our sins and mistakes never comes easily. But the Holy Spirit will graciously reveal disordered loves in our lives—loves that have stolen our hearts from God—so we can repent and receive God's righteousness.

Instead of clinging to our shiny idols or man-made gods, let's repent of our false worship.

Receive. Receive God's forgiveness and the gentle rain of His righteousness.

Even in the middle of Israel's horrific unfaithfulness, God offers a beautiful promise:

> Sow for yourselves righteousness;
> reap steadfast love;
> break up your fallow ground,
> for it is the time to seek the LORD,
> that He may come and rain righteousness upon you.
> (Hosea 10:12)

Although Israel won't pay attention to God's words until after their time of punishment and exile, God says He will come to them again. When they have returned and repented, He will rain righteousness on their hearts and make them clean again. They will reap—gather for their very own—His unceasing love.

God speaks these words to us as well. We can't gain righteousness on our own. Our sinful nature continually pulls us toward counterfeit gods. Our job is to ask God to help us identify those idols. To pray He will break up the hard, fallow ground of our hearts, pull out the weeds of stubbornness and pride, yank out the thorns and thistles of false loves. As the Holy Spirit leads us to repentance, we seek God again. We receive the gentle rain of Christ's righteousness on our souls.

Just like the friend who told my sister she didn't know how to choose a man, our sinful hearts will always have the tendency to choose the wrong gods. Time and again, we will discover that we have given our hearts away to false pursuits, relationships, or treasures. Like me, you may need to repent of the same idol over and over.

But just as David pursued Shelly, arranging his schedule to meet her every morning, God persistently pursues us. He never gives up on us, even when we try to avoid Him and His Word. He promises that if we will only come back to Him and allow His Spirit to soften our hearts, He will rain His righteousness on us. He will shower His steadfast, unchanging love on our thirsty souls.

LIVE LIKE YOU'RE LOVED

When we read this section of Hosea, we may cringe at the harsh words of judgment. We don't usually highlight and memorize passages of Law and punishment. When is the last time you saw a meme saying "For you have played the whore, forsaking your God" (Hosea 9:1) shared on social media? But the words of Hosea give us a window into the heart of God, the God who chose Israel as His very own and the God who gave His Son to bring us into His family.

Picture a loving husband who notices his wife pulling away from him. When he leans in to kiss her, she deliberately moves aside. When he reaches out to her at night, she turns her back to him and goes to sleep.

Oh, she still takes advantage of his income and provision. He looks at the credit card statement and sees the shoes, bags, and clothes she purchases every month. He notices visits to restaurants. And his heart drops when he reads charges to fancy hotels—hotels where he didn't stay.

Consider this scenario as a picture of how God feels when we pull away from Him. One commentator wrote, "Doesn't our God care about us at least as much as a faithful husband cares about his wife?"[50] When we read Hosea, we see the record of Israel's unfaithful actions and the broken heart of Yahweh. God wept at how His people turned their back on Him and pursued false loves.

To live like you're loved by almighty God means to grasp His passion for you. To see His desire to have an exclusive relationship with you. To understand His hurting heart when competing lovers capture your attention.

Although the false loves of our culture promise satisfaction, nothing can fill our hearts like the tender affection of God.

When we appreciate the depths of Jesus' affection for us, we can better ignore the lure of counterfeit loves. Although the false loves of our culture promise satisfaction, nothing can fill our hearts like the tender affection of God. When the Holy Spirit moves us to abandon our worldly love affairs, we can repent and return to God's bottomless grace and relentless love.

CHAPTER SIX

A RELENTLESS LOVE STORY

Walter loved Edna for sixty-plus years—even when she couldn't love him back.

Oh, it didn't start out that way. They married young and had a lovely family. When the children grew up, Walter and Edna decided to make their lives easier by moving into senior housing. They made their apartment their own by bringing favorite furnishings and memorabilia from their home. Walter and Edna enjoyed the camaraderie of fun and games with fellow retirees.

But a few years into their time at the retirement center, friends began to notice something was a bit off with Edna's behavior. At times, she seemed forgetful and confused. Perhaps out of love for his wife, Walter tried to ignore the signs. But eventually, he admitted that Edna needed help. Visits to her doctor and repeated testing confirmed it: Edna had symptoms of Alzheimer's disease.

Unfortunately, the disease progressed rather quickly, and in eighteen months, Edna's forgetfulness had advanced to the point that she needed full-time nursing care. For the first time in decades, they each lived apart from the one they loved. Edna moved into a nursing home while Walter continued to live at the retirement apartment.

Yet even this couldn't keep them apart. Every day, weather permitting, Walter drove to the nursing home and sat with his wife for eight hours. He lovingly held her hand and shared life as best he could. However, as the fabric of Edna's memory continued to fray, sometimes she didn't remember Walter. She would pull away when this man she didn't recognize tried to hold her hand. Because he didn't want to make her feel uncomfortable, Walter had to be content merely sitting with her.

My pastor husband, John, visited this couple for years and often commented on Walter's devotion to a woman who could no longer reciprocate his love. John had witnessed their affection for each other when he visited both of them at the retirement home, and he couldn't help but marvel at Walter's continued devotion to his wife as her mind unraveled.

John once asked Walter if he ever thought of staying home instead of visiting Edna. With tears in his eyes, he said, "She is my *wife*." Even though participating in the activities at the retirement center might have been more interesting than spending another day at the bedside of a woman who might not know him that day, Walter continually showed up for Edna. His relentless love for his wife meant sticking with her for better or for worse.

Eventually, Edna succumbed to the disease and went home to heaven. Shortly thereafter, Walter, then in his nineties, developed serious health problems and needed full-time nursing care. He passed away a couple of months after his beloved wife.

God's Relentless Love Never Gives Up

Hosea 11

MEMORY VERSE

I led them with cords of kindness,
with the bands of love.

Hosea 11:4

Walter never gave up on Edna. Even when she could no longer respond to his love, he continued to visit her. Even when she could no longer act as the woman he first knew and married, he loved and cared for her.

Hosea 11 opens a window into God's heart, revealing that He feels the same way about His people. Yahweh continued to love Israel, even when she forgot her unique and intimate relationship with Him. He continued to reach out even though she willfully rejected Him and ran to other lovers. God had every right to abandon His chosen nation, but His caring heart wouldn't allow Him to do that.

We can embrace this good news for ourselves. At times, we may feel God could never forgive our horrendous past mistakes or that we have strayed so far from His love that He would never welcome us back. But the message of Hosea 11 reassures us that God never gives up on us.

At times, we may feel God could never forgive our horrendous past mistakes. But Hosea reassures us that God never gives up on us.

A GOD WHO NEVER GIVES UP

Hosea opens chapter 11 with God's own words: "When Israel was a child, I loved him" (v. 1). As one commentator wrote, "The Lord allows us to look right into his heart, to experience his feelings for his child Israel."[51] God's words remind me of someone reminiscing—recalling all the delightful moments *and* all the painful periods shared with a loved one.

First, God recalls how He took Israel out of captivity in Egypt and how He continually called out to them (see vv. 1–2). He remembers the good times when He guided them and taught them how to walk (see v. 3).

But Yahweh also remembers the heartrending times when His child repeatedly ran away from Him (see v. 5). He sighs, "My people are bent on turning away from Me" (v. 7a). Because of their rebellious, sinful nature, they repeatedly turn from God instead of toward Him. They might "call out to the Most High" (v. 7b), but He sees through their empty words and into their unrepentant hearts. Therefore, He won't hear Israel's cries. In previous chapters, we've heard all about their unfaithfulness—how they worshiped counterfeit gods. We've seen how they trusted foreign powers more than almighty God. We've witnessed how they adopted the sinful practices of the culture around them.

Even though His people have hurt Him over and again, God doesn't want to abandon His people. His tender heart recalls how, in the past, He led them with "cords of kindness" (v. 4). But now, they continue to turn away, and He has no choice but to implement His punishment: "Assyria shall be their king" (v. 5). Israel's enemies will come with swords, break down the city gates, and attack the people because they trusted in "their own counsels" instead of Yahweh (v. 6).

However, even with all the pain Israel has caused Him, the Lord cannot completely abandon them. His heart "recoils" at the thought (v. 8b). The Hebrew word used here for "recoil," *haphak*, has the idea of being turned over.[52] God has every right to send His chosen people away forever, to quit loving them, to discard them like yesterday's lunch. Yet His heart shudders at the thought of such drastic measures.

Yahweh asks, "How can I give you up, O Ephraim? How can I hand you over, O Israel?" (v. 8a). The Lord's unwavering love won't allow Him to give up on His people.

ADMAH AND ZEBOIIM

In Hosea 11:8, God not only questions how He could ever give up on His people; He also asks: "How can I make you like Admah? How can I treat you like Zeboiim?" What is He talking about here? What or who are Admah and Zeboiim?

You may remember the Old Testament account of Sodom and Gomorrah—the cities God totally demolished because of their wickedness (see Genesis 19). Scripture tells us that the smaller nearby towns of Admah and Zeboiim suffered the same fate: "The whole land burned out with brimstone and salt, nothing sown and nothing growing, where no plant can sprout, an overthrow like that of Sodom and Gomorrah, Admah, and Zeboiim, which the LORD overthrew in His anger and wrath" (Deuteronomy 29:23).

Not only were Admah and Zeboiim destroyed, they were all but forgotten. In Hosea, God says He can't bring Himself to annihilate His beloved nation like He wiped out those wicked cities. He can't forget about them the way Admah and Zeboiim have slipped from memory.

Instead, God's "compassion grows warm and tender" (v. 8b). He could act in fury, but He doesn't behave like men who lash out in anger. He will not carry out His rage. God tells His rebellious children that He still remains "the Holy One in your midst" (v. 9). What a reassuring thought, especially after His earlier words, when He named Hosea's third child and said, "Call his name Not My People, for you are not My people, and I am not your God" (1:9).

God not only reminisces about the past, He sees into the future when His children will eventually come back to Him. He looks forward to the day when He will "return them to their homes" (11:11b). God gives this promise of mercy not for the people of Hosea's day but for their descendants.[53]

After the time of punishment, a remnant of Israel will return to God. They will come back trembling like birds (v. 11a). Although the destruction of the Northern Kingdom will be permanent, eventually, some of the people will return to settle in the land. This prophecy becomes reality in 539 BC, about two hundred years after Hosea, when Cyrus, king of Persia, allows people from both Israel and Judah to return to their homeland.[54]

THE FATE OF JUDAH

Hosea 11:12 describes both the Northern and Southern Kingdoms:

Ephraim has surrounded Me with lies,
and the house of Israel with deceit,
but Judah still walks with God
and is faithful to the Holy One.

Ephraim practiced deceit by calling out to Yahweh and worshiping other gods at the same time. From the very first king of Israel, who set up the calf idols at Dan and Bethel, up to Hosea's time, Israel's evil kings led the people astray. But south of the border, Judah had some kings who were faithful to the Lord (especially Josiah and Hezekiah). The godly influence of these kings enabled the Southern Kingdom of Judah to last 150 years longer than the Northern Kingdom.

YAHWEH'S EXPRESSIONS OF LOVE

Throughout the Book of Hosea, God uses marriage imagery to describe His love for His people. He explains His hurting heart in terms of a jilted lover.

But in chapter 11, God uses other analogies. Our human brains can't completely grasp the enormity of His love, so He uses multiple word pictures to help us comprehend His passion. One commentator writes, "God always communicates with us in terms we can understand. He condescends to our level. *Anthropopathism* means that God expresses His thoughts and emotions as a human being would."[55]

The Tender Love of a Father. God begins Hosea 11 by describing His love for Israel as the tender love of a father for his son. We can almost picture God as the parent of a high school student getting misty-eyed while selecting baby photos to display for the graduation party. Yahweh remembers Israel's early days, when He took him by the hand and taught the unsteady toddler how to walk. God says:

I led them with cords of kindness,
with the bands of love. (Hosea 11:4a)

He guided His people with ropes woven from love and kindness. Can you almost see God the Father bending over to gently hold the hands of His young son Israel as he takes his first steps? The same cords of kindness allowed God to bind His perfect Son to the cross for our sake.

The Compassion of an Animal Caretaker. God shifts the allegory again in the second half of verse 4:

And I became to them as one who eases the yoke
on their jaws,
and I bent down to them and fed them. (Hosea 11:4b)

God now describes Himself as one who thoughtfully provides for animals. Donkeys and oxen wear yokes when they pull a cart or drag a plow. But the yoke can interfere with an animal's ability to chew when it bends down to a trough to eat.[56] In this analogy, God doesn't intend to compare us to animals; rather, He portrays Himself as someone who sees an animal's difficulty, then stoops to lift the yoke and feed the creature. God uses this picture to help us understand His caring nature. He sees our problems and empathizes with our struggles. He stoops down to ease our troubles and feed our souls.

God sees our problems and empathizes with our struggles. He stoops down to ease our troubles and feed our souls.

The Mercy of a Judge. In Hosea 11, Yahweh also expresses His love in the illustration of a merciful judge. Hosea used courtroom imagery several times in previous chapters. Here in chapter 11, God appears as both prosecutor and judge as He prepares to pronounce the sentence. But Yahweh states, "I will not execute My burning anger" (v. 9). Instead, Jesus took their sin and ours and bore the brunt of Yahweh's smoldering rage for us.

The second half of chapter 11 passionately portrays God's love. According to human reason, He should deliver a death sentence to His sinful people. Instead, He outlines His plans to bring them back from exile and resettle them in the land.[57]

The Roar of a Lion. The final picture of God's love comes in a roar:

They shall go after the LORD;
  He will roar like a lion;
when He roars,
  His children shall come trembling from the west. (Hosea 11:10)

Lions mark their territory and proclaim their arrival with a roar. Yahweh's metaphorical roar announces that He has come again to His people and reestablished His rule.[58] The roar may seem terrifying, but it declares God's powerful love: "With the *roar of a lion* the Lord will declare both His inexorable wrath against sin and His inextinguishable love for His children; and at that roar His wayward children will at last *come trembling* home to Him. . . . That roar was ultimately heard at Calvary, and all history since then is the history of the homecoming of mankind."[59]

The marriage metaphor God used so often in Hosea speaks especially of the intimacy and devotion of God's love for us. But these other word pictures help us understand other aspects of His love: the tender love a father has for his infant son, the compassion an animal owner has for a helpless beast, the mercy of a judge who can't bring himself to condemn, the powerful love expressed in the roar of a lion.

God's Word applies to our lives as well, so hear it as if God were speaking directly to you:

I have always loved you. Ever since you became My child in the waters of Baptism, I have continually called out to you. Remember when you took your first steps of faith? Whenever you felt unsteady or wobbly, I held you with cords of kindness. When you started to stumble, I gripped you with bands of love.

When the work of this world exhausted you, I fed you with My Word and Sacraments. I eased the burden of the yoke so you could eat and be refreshed. I even got in the yoke with you so we could work together, and I could give you strength (see Matthew 11:28–30).

When the judgment of the Law condemned your sin, I sent Jesus to take your punishment. The Law pointed its finger to execute a sentence of eternal death. But I couldn't let that happen. As a just judge, I couldn't overlook your sin, yet My heart crumbled at the thought of losing you. So I sent My only Son to take the penalty of your wrongdoing. He bore My blazing anger so that you can return to Me. I am still "the Holy One in your midst" (Hosea 11:9).

If you hear My roar, remember that roar constantly calls out to you. It bellows, "Come back to Me. Let Me rule in your heart and mind. Come in awe of My power and reign, but realize that this power can protect you and restore you to your proper home—the kingdom of God."

GOD IS NOT A MAN

In Hosea 11:9, Yahweh declares, "I am God and not a man." The Lord uses human terms to describe Himself and His love, yet He makes the distinction that He is not like us. Sometimes we imagine God as someone just a bit bigger than ourselves. We define Him in terms of our desires and assumptions. But in reality, God is more powerful, more holy, more majestic, more awesome than we can ever imagine. While He created us in His image, and we share some of His qualities, our puny minds cannot grasp His greatness—yet.

GOD'S COVENANT LOVE

When we read Hosea 11, we can sense God's sorrow and disappointment. We can almost hear the sadness in His voice in this paraphrase of verses 1–2: "Israel, I remember when you were a toddler, and I led you by the hand. My love guided you through dry deserts and enemy lands. But when you got older, like a rebellious teenager, you turned away from me."

Israel's revolt disappointed Yahweh, but it didn't surprise Him. As omniscient God, He knew all along that His children would rebel. Even as He led the infant nation with cords of kindness and gently taught him how to walk, Yahweh could see ahead to the time when His beloved child would reject His affection.

In fact, the Lord made provisions for this time of rebellion in His original covenant with the people as they were about to enter the Promised Land. Hosea's words echo the words of God through Moses in Deuteronomy:

> When you father children and children's children, and have grown old in the land, if you act corruptly by making a carved image in the form of anything, and by doing what is evil in the sight of the LORD your God, so as to provoke Him to anger, I call heaven and earth to witness against you today, that you

will soon utterly perish from the land that you are going over the Jordan to possess. You will not live long in it, but will be utterly destroyed. And the LORD will scatter you among the peoples, and you will be left few in number among the nations where the LORD will drive you. And there you will serve gods of wood and stone, the work of human hands, that neither see, nor hear, nor eat, nor smell. (Deuteronomy 4:25–28)

From the very beginning, God warned the Israelites against making a carved image. But what did the Israelites do? They constructed golden calves to worship. As they were about to enter the Promised Land, Yahweh warned that provoking His anger through the worship of false gods would result in their removal from that land. Centuries later, God now delivers their eviction notice. In Deuteronomy 4, God warns that their population will dwindle and be scattered among the nations (see v. 27). In Hosea, God assures them that the enemy will soon arrive and "devour them because of their own counsels" (11:6). Some people will flee to Egypt. Most will be taken to Assyria (see v. 5).

But this doesn't mean the end of Israel. God looks ahead even further to the time when His people will seek Him again. Moses wrote:

But from there you will seek the LORD your God and you will find Him, if you search after Him with all your heart and with all your soul. When you are in tribulation, and all these things come upon you in the latter days, you will return to the LORD your God and obey His voice. For the LORD your God is a merciful God. He will not leave you or destroy you or forget the covenant with your fathers that He swore to them. (Deuteronomy 4:29–31)

The merciful God peers into the future, when His beloved nation will once again pursue Him fervently and wholeheartedly. Yahweh promises He will never abandon them or forget about them.

In Hosea, God reaffirms this hope:

His children shall come trembling from the west;
they shall come trembling like birds from Egypt,
 and like doves from the land of Assyria,
 and I will return them to their homes, declares the LORD.
(Hosea 11:10b–11)

When I read these passages, I sometimes wonder why God bothered with Israel at all. If He knew His beloved would break His heart, why did He choose them as His special people? Why did He care for them in the wilderness and give them the Promised Land? Wouldn't it have caused a lot less trouble to simply never involve Himself in messy human relationships?

To our human point of view, perhaps this seems correct. But Yahweh's covenant relationship with Israel has always served as a picture of God's relationship with all mankind. Even as the Lord knew Israel would shun His love when He first called them as His chosen people, He knew that mankind would reject Him when He placed Adam and Eve in the Garden of Eden. So why did He create humans?

While we can never fully understand the mind of God, we know God is love (see 1 John 4:16), and love requires an object. His very character desired someone to love. But in this love, He also desired love in return, so He created man in His own image. He gave humans the ability to respond to His love or reject it. Even while He pushed together some clay to form Adam, God the Father knew He would eventually need to sacrifice His perfect Son to save sinful people. And He did it anyway. He created us so we could be with Him forever to praise and glorify Him in heaven (see Revelation 4:11).

Even while He pushed together some clay to form Adam, God the Father knew He would eventually need to sacrifice His perfect Son to save sinful people. And He did it anyway.

How humbling to realize that even though God the Father knew I would frequently mess up, He still created me. Even though I would sometimes choose to worship success instead of Him, He brought me into the world. Even though I would occasionally forget about Him completely, He still loved me enough to send Jesus to the cross to rescue me.

LIVE LIKE YOU'RE LOVED

When you feel you have messed up too much to be forgiven or wandered too far to be welcomed back, remember God's words to the sinful, rebellious nation of Israel:

> How can I give you up, O Ephraim?
> How can I hand you over, O Israel? (Hosea 11:8)

God's compassionate heart didn't allow Him to ditch Israel in the dust bin. His mercy will not allow Him to give up on you.

As humans, we occasionally need to give up on other people. A few years ago, when a close friend moved away, I hoped we would stay in touch. Maybe lunch dates could turn into phone calls and meetings over coffee could translate into emails and texts. So I tried phoning my friend—no answer. I attempted emails—no response. I sent texts—no reply. Eventually, I had to recognize that this friend had moved on. Her busy life in the new location didn't have room for old acquaintances. To accept this, I had to give up attempting to keep the relationship alive.

I imagine that God often feels like I did when He calls out to His children and they don't respond. He sends love letters in His Word, but they don't open them. He sends blessings on their lives, but they don't recognize that the gifts come from Him. He whispers His love in the brilliant blue sky and the morning dew on the grass, but the objects of His love rush through their days without noticing. Constantly having His love ignored must hurt much more than never attempting to love at all. If God were human, He would be tempted to give up.

At times, giving up on a human relationship is the logical and even healthy thing for us to do (especially if this relationship has become abusive). When we see the other person no longer has interest in a friendship, when we realize a potential romantic interest doesn't reciprocate our feelings or has different values, we need to move on. But God sees our relationship with Him as permanent as a lifelong marriage. His loving nature will not allow Him to wash His hands of His creation. He told Israel, and, to paraphrase Hosea 11:8, He tells us, "How can I give up on you? My heart cringes at the thought!" God will continue to reach out with cords of kindness and bands of love in hopes that we will eventually respond to the Holy Spirit's leading and grasp onto that love and kindness.

This truth reassures us when we've wandered from God's grace. Remember God's unfailing love when your past sins fill your soul with shame. When guilt weighs down your heart. When you feel God could never forgive you for the times you've ignored Him.

The relentless character of God's love also comforts us when we see family and friends repeatedly push Him away. Even when people dear to us seem to reject God's loving kindness, we can be sure that He still tugs on their hearts and whispers His mercy. As long as they walk the earth, the Lord will continue to pursue their hearts.

IMPENITENT HEARTS

Although God continually pursues us, He doesn't automatically welcome everyone into heaven. The apostle Paul wrote, "Do you presume on the riches of His kindness and forbearance and patience, not knowing that God's kindness is meant to lead you to repentance? But because of your hard and impenitent heart you are storing up wrath for yourself on the day of wrath when God's righteous judgment will be revealed" (Romans 2:4–5). The Lord keeps reaching out in kindness and mercy, but if we completely reject Him and refuse to trust Him before we die, He reluctantly agrees to live apart from us for all eternity.

Walter and Edna's story at the beginning of this chapter reflects the relentless love of God. Even when Edna no longer recognized Walter as the love of her long life, he still sat with her and held her hand. Even when we don't recognize God's tenacious love, He still holds us with bands of love (see Hosea 11:4). Like Walter—who never gave up on his wife, even when she could no longer function as the woman he married—God doesn't give up on us because of our weakness. He never abandons us because of our imperfections. In 2 Timothy 2:13, Paul says, "If we are faithless, He remains faithful—for He cannot deny Himself."

God perseveres, pursues, persists, and presses on—not because we are good, but because He is God.

God will never just move on and look for someone else. He never gives up on us. Even when we forget Him. Even when we worship counterfeit gods. Even when we chase other loves. Even when we are helpless. He will continually reach out in love, hoping we will trust in the mercy and grace He extends to us because of Jesus.

God perseveres, pursues, persists, and presses on—not because we are good but because He is God. Live confident in His relentless love.

CHAPTER SEVEN

A RELENTLESS LOVE STORY

"I could always count on my mom," my cousin Donna told me. "She attended every 4-H event and every organ recital. We took craft classes and learned how to macramé together." Donna grew up on a dairy farm in Wisconsin, so her family shared more togetherness than most. Milking seventy-five cows meant hours together in the barn every morning and evening. Summer brought days of working as a family in the fields. Donna always felt a sense of love and belonging—especially with her mother, my aunt Arlene.

But now the roles have shifted. Donna's father died about ten years ago, and a year later, doctors diagnosed her mother with congestive heart failure. Donna still lives on the farm with her husband and two children, so the backbreaking work of dairy farming became their responsibility.

Not only have work responsibilities changed, family roles have also shifted. In the past few years, my aunt Arlene has gradually shown signs of dementia. At first, she merely seemed a little more forgetful. But eventually, conversations became difficult as Arlene repeated the same topics over and over. As her brain slowly loses its ability to function, the parent-child roles reverse. Donna must prepare all the meals. She takes care of the household. At mealtimes, she tells her mother to clear her craft projects from the table so they can eat. Donna has to insist that her mother take a shower because sometimes Arlene acts like a toddler who dislikes baths.

Donna tells me, "It's been hard to switch roles. I don't want to tell my own mother what to do. But I have to do what is best for her, even if she doesn't like it. The doctor tells me that for many of us, we are once an adult and twice a child. My mother no longer acts like a grown-up; she acts like a kid."

The past few years have held heartache upon heartache. Falling milk prices made it necessary for the family to give up dairy farming. Although they still have some beef cows, they sold their dairy herd. Donna's husband has a heart condition that prevents him from working off the farm right now, so Donna and their two grown children have jobs to support the family.

At first, Donna felt she could leave her mother alone for a few hours each day, but a few months ago, Arlene needed to have her gallbladder removed. Infection set in and Arlene spent weeks in the hospital. The time in bed left her weak, and ever since then, her dementia has accelerated its downward spiral. A few weeks ago, Arlene fell in the bathroom and couldn't get up. Fortunately, Donna's son, Joe, was able to lift her off the floor, and although Arlene bumped her head on the tub, she seemed no worse for the experience. Yet when Donna's brother visited a few hours later and asked Arlene about her fall, she responded, "When did I fall?"

Because Donna feels she can no longer leave Arlene alone, she has had to give up her job. She devotes her time to taking care of her mother. Donna said, "I hope I can continue to keep her home until she goes home to heaven."

Donna has given up her own life and preferences. She devotes her time to taking care of her mother. She does it out of relentless love.

God's Relentless Love Disciplines

Hosea 12–13

But I am the LORD your God
from the land of Egypt;
you know no God but Me,
and besides Me there is no savior.

Hosea 13:4

Donna doesn't want the role of mothering her mother. She hates having to tell Arlene to do something Arlene doesn't want to do. But as Donna says, she needs to do what is best for her mother, even if her mother can no longer understand the purpose or reasoning.

In much the same way, Yahweh doesn't want to discipline His beloved nation. He would much rather continue to bless instead of punish. But Israel no longer listens to God's words of love, no longer understands the purpose of faithfulness. So even though the Lord never stops pursuing His beloved, never ceases to love His children, sometimes He needs to discipline them. In chapters 12 and 13 of Hosea, we see that the time of judgment has come. God persistently courted His people and called them His own, yet they continued to reject Him as their one and only. Israel's infidelity reached the tipping point.

We saw in Hosea 4 that the prophet's ministry to Israel lasted many years. Commentators surmise that the prophet wrote the twelfth and thirteenth chapters during King Hoshea's reign, near the end of the Northern Kingdom (see timeline on pages 12–13). Throughout the Book of Hosea, we have heard God's words of both judgment and grace, but chapters 12

119

and 13 contain few tender expressions of love. Like a parent who knows he must discipline his son for his own good, God knows He must punish Israel in the hope that someday His beloved will return to Him and the relationship will be restored.

ISRAEL'S INFIDELITY CONTRASTED WITH GOD'S FAITHFULNESS

Last Sunday, I chatted with a young couple during our congregation's after-service coffee hour. As we talked, they looked around and saw three of their four children snacking on the treats. But the seven-year-old, their eldest, wasn't in the room.

"She's probably playing with the other kids," I reassured them.

"Yeah," the dad agreed. "We don't worry too much about that one."

"She seems like the typical oldest child who likes to please her parents," I observed.

"Yep. On the other hand, this one"—he pointed at the two-year-old eating grapes—"has no such ambitions."

The nation of Israel constantly acted like an unruly toddler with no desire to please her God. In this section of Hosea, Yahweh recounts the whole history of the nation, underlining the times she rejected His love and disobeyed His commands.

The Lord begins by going all the way back to the nation's origins—their patriarch Jacob:

> The LORD has an indictment against Judah
>> and will punish Jacob according to his ways;
>> He will repay him according to his deeds.
> In the womb he took his brother by the heel,
>> and in his manhood he strove with God.
> He strove with the angel and prevailed;
>> he wept and sought His favor.
> He met God at Bethel,
>> and there God spoke with us. (Hosea 12:2–4)

You may remember that Jacob was a twin, and that, born second, he came out of the womb holding his brother's heel. His parents named him *Jacob*, which means "he takes by the heel," or "he cheats."[60] Indeed, Jacob did cheat Esau out of the birthright and blessing his brother deserved as the firstborn.

You can bet Esau's anger boiled over when he found out about Jacob's deception, and Jacob realized he had better leave! On his flight from his irate brother, Jacob "met God at Bethel" (v. 4). There, Yahweh gave him a dream of a ladder going up to heaven with angels ascending and descending. God stood above the ladder and said, "Behold, I am with you and will keep you wherever you go, and will bring you back to this land. For I will not leave you until I have done what I have promised you" (Genesis 28:15).

After the dream, Jacob continued on his way to his uncle Laban's home, where he lived for at least fourteen years, tending Laban's sheep. While there, he married Laban's daughters Leah and Rachel, and the Lord blessed them with children. (You can read the whole story about this dysfunctional family in Genesis 29–30.) Eventually, Jacob left his uncle's home in Paddan-aram, and, just as Yahweh promised he would, Jacob returned to Canaan.

Just before he reached the land of Canaan, however, Jacob engaged in an all-night wrestling match with someone who entered his camp. During this marathon event, Jacob realized the other wrestler was no ordinary man. He must have wondered, *Who is this mystery man—an angel? God Himself?* When Luther wrote about this incident, he said, "The wrestler is the Lord of glory, God Himself, or God's Son, who was to become incarnate and who appeared and spoke to the fathers."[61] Centuries after the wrestling match, Hosea wrote that Jacob "strove with God. He strove with the angel and prevailed" (Hosea 12:3–4).

Now, it's not every day that one wrestles with God, so Jacob pleaded with Him not to leave until God blessed him (see Genesis 32:26). Then the Lord said, "Your name shall no longer be called Jacob, but Israel, for you have striven with God and with men, and have prevailed" (v. 28). God changed Jacob's name from "cheat" to "he strives with God."[62] Through this name change, He commended Israel as someone who wrestled with God and by faith asked for the Lord's blessing.

Hosea retells the story of Israel's patriarch and namesake because the nation no longer acts like him. They don't strive for Yahweh's blessing—they seek out other gods and other sources of help. They have ignored the Lord by worshiping idols and offering sacrifices in places other than God's temple in Jerusalem (see Hosea 12:11). They made "metal images, idols skillfully made of their silver" (13:2a). In acts of worship, they kissed the false gods and even offered human sacrifices (see v. 2b).

Next, God recalls how He gave them kings when they wanted to be like the surrounding nations. Even though they rejected Him as their only

EPHRAIM FEEDS ON THE WIND

Ephraim feeds on the wind
 and pursues the east wind all day long;
they multiply falsehood and violence;
 they make a covenant with Assyria,
and oil is carried to Egypt. (Hosea 12:1)

Here the prophet uses the word *wind* in two ways. First, he states that the rebellious nation "feeds on the wind"—its spiritual food has no value. Worshiping idols and false gods only leaves the people empty. Second, Hosea tells us they pursue "the east wind all day long." Here, the "east wind" refers to Assyria, whom the Israelite kings asked for help. Assyrian annals record that King Hoshea paid ten talents of gold and a thousand talents of silver as tribute. Hoshea also sent a large quantity of olive oil to Egypt. Olives were not grown in Egypt, making this commodity very valuable.[63] But none of Hoshea's attempts to save Israel actually accomplished his purpose. Instead of chasing the wind, he should have pursued God.

sovereign, He gave them what they wanted. Now their kings have proven useless against their enemies (see 13:10–11). The Assyrians locked up Hoshea, the last king of the Northern Kingdom, and invaded the land (see 2 Kings 17:4–5).

Throughout this passage, Yahweh contrasts Israel's infidelity with His faithfulness. He brought them out of Egypt (see Hosea 12:9). He spoke with them through prophets (see v. 10), calling out to them to return. He has been the only Savior they have ever known (see 13:4). He knew them in the wilderness and provided for them in that dry land (see vv. 5–6). Now Yahweh longs for the time when they will one day return to Him and wait trustingly (see 12:6).

But God's chosen people continue to reject Him. The time for judgment has come.

PROSPERITY, PRIDE, AND FORGETFULNESS

When God reminded His people of all He had done for them, He also pointed out the results of His blessings:

> It was I who knew you in the wilderness,
> in the land of drought;
> but when they had grazed, they became full,
> they were filled, and their heart was lifted up;
> therefore they forgot Me. (Hosea 13:5–6)

Instead of responding in gratitude to all God had given them, they became full and content. Under King Jeroboam II, the nation expanded and became wealthy. But the people didn't give God the credit for this prosperity. Instead, "their heart was lifted up," and they became proud. The people wrongly assumed they had achieved success on their own. In Hosea 12:8, the prophet writes, "Ephraim has said, 'Ah, but I am rich; I have found wealth for myself.'"

But worst of all, in their prosperity, the people forgot God. They enjoyed the good gifts but totally ignored the Giver. Recently, I heard a sad story of an acquaintance who worked hard to provide for his family. Because of his success in the business world, they had a large, comfortable home and wanted for nothing. But his wife lost interest in him. She took advantage of the opulent lifestyle her husband provided but completely shut him out of her life, spending time with friends but never with him. Eventually, the wife asked for a divorce, even though the husband wanted to work on the marriage. Like this ungrateful wife, Israel enjoyed all the blessings of her relationship with her Husband, Yahweh (see 2:16), but turned her back on Him.

The people of Israel enjoyed the good gifts but totally ignored the Giver.

The Israelites even took prosperity and wealth as a sign that God approved of their lifestyle. The people said, "In all my labors they cannot find in me iniquity or sin" (12:8). Ancient cultures viewed financial success as a sign of divine favor.[64] The people of Israel felt they could do no wrong. "Ephraim was so steeped in sin that its people had convinced themselves that they had acquired their wealth justly."[65] But clearly, this was not the case. Through the prophet Hosea, God accused them of using false balances and oppression as a means to increase their riches (v. 7).

When the nation of Israel stood at the entrance of the Promised Land, Moses warned the people of the danger of prosperity:

> Take care lest you forget the LORD your God by not keeping His commandments and His rules and His statutes, which I command you today, lest, when you have eaten and are full and have built good houses and live in them, and when your herds and flocks multiply and your silver and gold is multiplied and all that you have is multiplied, then your heart be lifted up, and you forget the LORD your God, who brought you out of the land of Egypt, out of the house of slavery.
> (Deuteronomy 8:11–14)

Let's avoid the example of the Israelites and guard against the danger of forgetting God when times are good. When I'm struggling with my work—when piano students have quit or words simply won't come when I sit down to write—I'm sending up SOS prayers. I desperately cry out for God's help. But when my students arrive well practiced for lessons, my current writing project progresses, and life generally hums along, I may think, *I've got this*. Subconsciously, I may forget my desperate need for God. I spend less time in prayer when I should devote more time to praising the God of provision and thanking Him for His blessings.

At the entrance to the Promised Land, Moses also saw the hazardous possibility of pride and arrogance:

> Beware lest you say in your heart, "My power and the might
> of my hand have gotten me this wealth." You shall remember
> the LORD your God, for it is He who gives you power to get
> wealth, that He may confirm His covenant that He swore to
> your fathers, as it is this day. (Deuteronomy 8:17–18)

These words apply to us as well. When we have a job that pays the bills, when we have money in the bank, when we enjoy good food and a comfortable home, we may also think, *My intelligence, my ingenuity, my hard work have gotten me this far. The long hours I spent at the office and the sacrifices I made have finally paid off.* Although hard work and dedication definitely play a part in our finances and successes, we sometimes forget that God has given us the talents and aptitudes needed to complete our tasks. He gives us opportunities for education and employment.

Years ago, my husband and I built the home we currently own. While we had a lot of professionals working on the house, we acted as general contractors. My husband, John, spent weeks on the roof nailing down shingles. We installed insulation inside the walls and later painted those walls. I stained and varnished a mile of wood trim, and John installed it all. We could take credit for the house and think our skill and ingenuity gave us the home we have today.

But in truth, God provided so much for us. Our congregation sold us the property at a reduced rate. God supplied a contractor who not only framed the house but taught John how to install the roof, insulation, cabinets, hardwood floors, and wood trim. We didn't know the first thing about building a home, yet because of God's provision, subcontractors didn't steal us blind and the final product hasn't fallen apart. We may want to take the credit, but our home is actually a blessing from God. Let's all guard against the danger of taking credit for our prosperity.

WORDS OF JUDGMENT

Because of Israel's forgetfulness of all God has done for them, because of their unfaithfulness, Yahweh now declares that the time has come for punishment. The Book of Hosea repeatedly uses the marriage relationship as the predominant image of God's love. Throughout the centuries, Yahweh pursued His people, calling out to them in love and desiring nothing more than their undivided devotion. And from the beginning, God warned them that He is a jealous God. When He gave Moses the Ten Commandments, He said:

> You shall not make for yourself a carved image, or any likeness of anything that is in heaven above, or that is in the earth beneath, or that is in the water under the earth. You shall not bow down to them or serve them, for I the LORD your God am a jealous God, visiting the iniquity of the fathers on the children to the third and the fourth generation of those who hate Me. (Exodus 20:4–5)

Although we think of jealousy as a negative emotion, the Hebrew word *ganna* can also mean "zealous" or "passionate." God prohibited the worship of other gods because a good marriage has only two parties. All other lovers must be excluded.[66] God's powerful and righteous desire for the faithfulness of His people meant that He couldn't continue to ignore their illicit behavior.

God prohibited the worship of other gods because a good marriage has only two parties. All other lovers must be excluded.

Perhaps the people thought punishment would never come. Maybe they saw Yahweh as a parent who threatened a time-out for bad behavior but never enforced it. So they persisted in their worship of Baal. They continued their cultic prostitution at the Asherah poles.

But now God declares, "Enough!" In Hosea 12 and 13, we see the climax of His message of judgment: "The wrath of God against the people who have broken his covenant is here portrayed with intensity unmatched elsewhere in Hosea."[67] Yahweh uses strong words of punishment.

Bloodguilt. "Ephraim has given bitter provocation; so his Lord will leave his bloodguilt on him and will repay him for his disgraceful deeds" (12:14). In Leviticus 20:10–16, God describes the punishments for sexual immorality with the words "their blood is upon them." Adulterers received a death sentence.

Death. "When Ephraim spoke, there was trembling; he was exalted in Israel, but he incurred guilt through Baal and died" (Hosea 13:1). Israel had experienced glory days with prosperity and military strength. Ephraim was the most prominent tribe in the Northern Kingdom. One famous Ephraimite, Jeroboam I, became the first king of the Northern Kingdom.[68] But when he instituted the worship of Baal, he brought a death sentence to his nation.

Obliteration. "Therefore they shall be like the morning mist or like the dew that goes early away, like the chaff that swirls from the threshing floor or like smoke from a window" (v. 3). Mist and dew disappear as soon as the sun appears. Chaff, the light and inedible part of grain, blows away in the wind as the thresher throws the grain into the air, leaving the edible part to settle back to the threshing floor. Smoke escaped from a window because houses in ancient times did not have chimneys.[69] All these images demonstrated how quickly and completely Israel would be destroyed when God executed His judgment.

Violent Destruction. "So I am to them like a lion; like a leopard I will lurk beside the way. I will fall upon them like a bear robbed of her cubs; I will tear open their breast, and there I will devour them like a lion, as a wild beast would rip them open" (vv. 7–8). We don't want to imagine God as a dangerous lion, a lurking leopard, or an irate mother bear whose cubs are missing, but these images let us glimpse the severity of God's anger when we reject His grace. His intense fury is just as true as His relentless love.[70]

Pangs of Childbirth. "The iniquity of Ephraim is bound up; his sin is kept in store. The pangs of childbirth come for him, but he is an unwise son, for at the right time he does not present himself at the opening of the womb" (vv. 12–13). God compares the pain the Israelites will experience to the pain of childbirth. However, this experience will not end happily because Ephraim wastes the opportunity for new birth by refusing to repent.[71]

Agricultural Disaster. "Though he may flourish among his brothers, the east wind, the wind of the LORD, shall come, rising from the wilderness, and his fountain shall dry up; his spring shall be parched; it shall strip his treasury of every precious thing" (v. 15). The name *Ephraim* means "fruitfulness," but now the land will dry up.[72] Sometimes the Bible references a withering east wind from the desert that dried up plants (see Genesis 41:6; Ezekiel 17:10), but here, the east wind is also a metaphor for Assyria, God's instrument for destruction. The Assyrians invaded Israel in 734 BC and totally defeated its people in 722 BC, leaving the land barren for decades.[73]

Horrors of War. "Samaria shall bear her guilt, because she has rebelled against her God; they shall fall by the sword; their little ones shall be dashed in pieces, and their pregnant women ripped open" (Hosea 13:16). Because of the people's rebellion, God allowed the Assyrians to attack Israel. Their siege of the capital city, Samaria, lasted three years (see 2 Kings 17:5). The ruthless Assyrians probably employed every cruel war practice available, and we know that the appalling practice of cutting

Hosea in the New Testament

Chapters 12 and 13 of Hosea contain dire words of judgment. But even in this passage, we find one more Law-Gospel contrast. God surprises us with a message of condemnation, followed by words of grace. Right after He tells Ephraim that the coming punishment will be as painful as the pains of childbirth, the Lord says:

I shall ransom them from the power of Sheol;
I shall redeem them from Death.
O Death, where are your plagues?
O Sheol, where is your sting?
Compassion is hidden from My eyes. (Hosea 13:14)

Although God's compassion is hidden for now, the Israelites can hear hope in the words *ransom* and *redeem.* In the future, God Himself will pay the price to rescue all who trust in Him.[74]

The apostle Paul quoted this verse in 1 Corinthians:

When the perishable puts on the imperishable, and
the mortal puts on immortality, then shall come to
pass the saying that is written:

"Death is swallowed up in victory."
"O death, where is your victory?
O death, where is your sting?" (1 Corinthians 15:54–55)

Israel deserved the punishment it received. We, too, deserve a death sentence for our sin. But God's grace reverses the sentence. The old covenant promised punishment for the unfaithful and death to the disobedient. But in the new covenant, Jesus brings victory over death. He met the requirement of the Law and took the penalty we deserved. Now physical death is the means to eternal life with the One who loves us.

open pregnant women did occur in ancient times (see 2 Kings 15:16; Amos 1:13). Can you imagine the horror husbands experienced as they watched the mutilation of their wives or the slaughter of their children? If only the people had returned and repented—God still longed to be their savior (see Hosea 13:4).

WAIT CONTINUALLY

As I look at Hosea's ominous message to the Israelites and witness their rejection of God's grace, I am reminded that I don't want to act like them. God called out to His people for centuries. He patiently waited for them to return to Him, but they refused and missed the opportunity for God's rescue. God cries out to us as well:

> So you, by the help of your God, return,
>> hold fast to love and justice,
>> and wait continually for your God. (Hosea 12:6)

First, God pleads with us to return to Him. When we've turned to other loves to make us feel better about ourselves, God doesn't push us away. When we've become infatuated with the world or listened to Satan's seductive suggestions, God still asks us to come back. And we don't even have to do this by ourselves. In fact, we *can't* do it on our own—we do it only with the help of God the Holy Spirit working in our hearts, giving us the power to repent.

Second, the Lord tells us to "hold fast to love and justice." These two words characterize God. As a just God, He cannot ignore sin. Although He patiently waited for Israel to return to Him, He eventually needed to punish their unfaithfulness. We, too, deserve punishment. But in love, God sent His Son, Jesus, to take our sentence of death and damnation. When we hold fast to love and justice, we remember the penalty we deserve and how God's love rescued us from that eternal punishment.

Third, Hosea tells us to "wait continually for your God." This Old Testament phrase means to patiently trust God to act.[75] The Israelite nation thought their prosperity depended on their own efforts, but Hosea told the people that instead of worshiping idols, instead of sacrificing to multiple gods, all they needed to do was wait. The Hebrew word for "wait," *qavah*, means "to expect or look eagerly for."[76] The Israelites should have *expected* Yahweh to provide for them. After all, He had rescued them from slavery and from the Egyptian army and had fed them with manna for forty years!

God asks us also to trust Him—to constantly, perpetually wait for Him to act in our lives. When we begin to doubt that He will come through, we can look to the pages of the Bible for examples of His faithfulness. We can recall times in our own lives when God has generously provided. We can remember that His absolute faithfulness will give us everything we need in heaven, even if we don't see all our desires met here on earth.

> God asks us also to trust Him—to constantly, perpetually wait for Him to act in our lives.

LIVE LIKE YOU'RE LOVED

Hosea tells the story of unfaithful Israel's persistent rejection of Yahweh's relentless love. To get their attention, God used drastic measures. Like my cousin Donna, who sometimes makes decisions in her mother's best interest, even though Arlene may not like them, God decided to allow Assyria to destroy His beloved nation in hopes that some of the people would return to His love. He disciplined His people.

Discipline doesn't feel like love. (Ask any kid who has been grounded for a week!) But Hebrews 12:6 reminds us, "For the Lord disciplines the one He loves, and chastises every son whom He receives." God disciplines out of His never-failing love for us.

When we, like the Israelites, experience difficult circumstances, we need to examine our lives to see if we have brought on these challenging conditions through our bad choices, rejection of God's ways, or pursuit of false loves. But *paideuō*—the Greek word for "discipline" used in

Hebrews 12:6—means "training" and "education" and demonstrates that sometimes God uses discipline for instruction and not for punishment. While God disciplined the Israelites because of their disobedience, not all discipline is punitive.

When tough times come, we may wonder, *Does God still love me?* Just like the ancient Israelites, we tend to equate blessings with love and hardship with displeasure. We need to remember that not every earthly setback comes from God's hand. Sometimes we suffer as a result of the sins of others or simply from living in a broken world. But God can use even these tragedies for good. Dear friends, remember that God disciplines the one He *loves.* The painful experiences may not be punishment but a means to draw you closer. Trials remind us how desperately we need our Father, our Savior, our Comforter.

When we experience hardship, we remember that He disciplines out of His relentless love and that He turns all things to good for those who love Him.

Living like we're loved means that when we experience prosperity, we thank the God who provides everything we have. And when we experience hardship, we remember that He disciplines out of His relentless love and that He turns all things to good for those who love Him. Christ continually invites us to return to His loving arms, to draw near to Him in the Sacrament, and rejoice in the life and salvation He gives there.

CHAPTER EIGHT

A RELENTLESS LOVE STORY

Heidi and Jim liked to say they grew up on the same block in two different cities. Heidi, from Wisconsin, and Jim, a native Ohioan, met on a college campus in Illinois on a 90-degree day, right after Heidi had finished a three-mile run. Dressed in gray sweats and "glistening" from the exertion, she didn't look like she had just stepped out of the pages of a fashion magazine. But they both felt an immediate connection.

Jim and Heidi married thirteen months after they met. They lived in a 700-square-foot apartment that was part of a dorm on the Concordia College—River Forest (now Concordia University Chicago) campus. There, Heidi worked as the resident director while Jim finished his bachelor's degree. Living in a college dormitory with two hundred students wouldn't qualify as an ideal home for most newlyweds, but they loved the students. During their fifteen years at the college, they both finished master's degrees, welcomed two children into the family, and developed lifelong friendships. (They also moved into a larger home when Heidi became director of residence life and later, assistant dean of students.)

Jim had long heard the calling to pastoral ministry, so in July of 1997, they moved to Fort Wayne, Indiana, so he could attend the seminary there. That same year, doctors diagnosed Jim with congestive heart failure and diabetes. He began a new journey: full-time student with health issues. Jim put exercise and dietary change front and center, yet five years later, he experienced three strokes. The strokes left him with left-side neglect, and so this dear, determined, learned, godly man learned to speak and walk again. In addition, his family learned how to help him—and not help him. Heidi says, "I learned how to take care of Jim because I had to and because I promised. Something about those weddings vows that say, 'For better or worse, richer or poorer, in sickness and in health.' Jim used to tease me that I picked him out of a scratch-and-dent sale, and I always responded, 'Yes, and I still would—every day of the week and twice on Sundays.'"

Unfortunately, the strokes were not the only issue. A few years later, Jim lost his left eye due to a medication anomaly—devastating for an avid reader. Then, kidney failure meant dialysis three times a week. Next, he lost his left leg due to a wound that would not heal. Heidi recalls thinking, *Really?! How much more for him?*

She adds, "There is no shame in admitting we all questioned God and this path. Yet, God provided hope and comfort. I specifically remember one April morning I felt I could no longer *do all of this!* and God's assurance came in the beauty of a pink tulip. You see, all of the perennials had been dug out of the front yard to make room for a handicap ramp. But one pink tulip—my favorite flower—survived and bloomed on the day I needed it most."

Jim's health continued to decline, and finally, there came a point when he declared he no longer wanted to be poked, prodded, tested, and hospitalized. He said, "Just make me comfortable." Heidi remembers everything about the night before his death on February 25, 2009. "Because it was Ash Wednesday, a dear friend asked our pastor to come to our home and give us Communion. I don't even have words to describe that experience. After our pastor left, we settled in. Jim was restless and remembering things from his past. He talked. I sang to him, talked with him, and made him promise if he saw Jesus' hand to take it—the kids and I would be okay. We woke the next morning, went through our morning routine. I kissed him, told him I loved him and went into the bathroom to wash my hands. When I came back to check on him, the Lord had taken him home peacefully. During this journey, I had often commented when

Jim headed off to surgery or treatment, He will either get better or per-fect. Alas, now he had become perfect."

When Heidi married Jim, she had no idea of the difficult road they would travel. She could have forgotten her marriage vows and aban-doned Jim, but her relentless love kept her at his side. Now she misses Jim every day. Their exceptional love affair inspired many, but Heidi says, "Our relentless love pales by comparison to the relentless love God has for us."

GOD'S RELENTLESS LOVE KNOWS NO BOUNDS

Hosea 14

MEMORY VERSE

I will love them freely.

Hosea 14:4

Heidi and Jim's relentless love story doesn't have the typical happily-ever-after ending we all long for. When they first met, all plotlines pointed to a fairy-tale conclusion of their girl-meets-boy story. But their romantic tale had more heartbreaking twists than they expected and an ending that arrived way too soon.

Don't we all want every love story to have a blissful ending? We want the girl to get the guy at the end of the movie. We hope all obstacles will be removed from the couple's path to happiness by the end of the book. We yearn for the perfect conclusion and feel cheated when we don't get it.

So do we get that feel-good conclusion at the end of Hosea? We do—and we don't. Hosea reminds the people of the love story Yahweh penned for them: almighty God chooses a lowly, backward nation to be His Bride. He provides lavish love and perfect provision for His beloved. But the nation rejects His love, chases other gods, and then falls on hard times. Hosea warns that unless they change their ways, punishment will come. They will endure exile and separation from the land they love.

In the final chapter of Hosea, we see both God's invitation to Israel to return to Him and His promise to love them freely. He paints a picture of what their lives will look like when they finally do come back to Him.

RETURN

Hosea 14 begins with the prophet's call to Israel:

Return, O Israel, to the LORD your God,
for you have stumbled because of your iniquity. (Hosea 14:1)

Hosea repeats God's desperate call to His beloved: "Return. Come back to Me. You've stumbled and lost your way, but I have never given up on you. It's not too late. Return." Can you hear God's passion for His people? He yearns for reconciliation. They have abandoned the One who longs for intimate relationship with His people. He cries out to them to come back to Him, but He never forces them. They must return on their own.

Hosea repeats God's desperate call to His beloved: "Return. Come back to Me."

That very word *return* is a key word in Hosea's message. He uses the Hebrew word *shub* twenty times in the book and three times in chapter 14 alone. *Shub* can be translated as "return" or "repent." Israel, the wayward bride, must admit her sins and change her ways in order to return.

Perhaps you know someone whose marriage shattered because of infidelity. The faithful spouse has every right to obtain a divorce. But maybe that spouse hopes to repair the relationship. Can reconciliation happen without the offending party admitting guilt and promising to change? Of course not. In the same way, Israel, the transgressor, must confess and repent.

Have you ever wanted to apologize but struggled to find just the right words? Hosea helps the Israelite people by telling them how to ask for forgiveness:

Take with you words
   and return to the LORD;
say to Him,
   "Take away all iniquity;
accept what is good,
   and we will pay with bulls
   the vows of our lips.
Assyria shall not save us;
   we will not ride on horses;
and we will say no more, 'Our God,'
   to the work of our hands.
In You the orphan finds mercy." (Hosea 14:2–3)

God has been longing to hear these words. He has waited and wait-ed for His beloved to confess her unfaithfulness and ask for forgiveness. He has wanted to hear the people's praise instead of watching the hypo-critical offering of bulls. He has hoped His beloved would recognize His saving power and the futility of going to foreign nations for help. He has yearned for the return to an exclusive relationship where His people give up their man-made gods.

God longs for all of His people to return. I, too, need to repent when I've strayed from His love, worshiped my own man-made gods, or trust-ed in the things of this world rather than in my heavenly Father. I need to "take . . . words" as an offering (v. 2). Hosea's words guide my own: "Jesus, Savior, take away my sin. Accept my repentance. I offer the sacri-fice of confession. I realize now that the world can't give me what I need. I can't get joy and peace through my own efforts. I know I've worshiped success and bowed at the altar of achievement, but I'm done with that. You are my God—the source of mercy for my needy soul."

LOVE THEM FREELY

When a marriage falls apart because of a spouse's unfaithfulness, there is no guarantee it can be repaired. Even if the spouse who strayed apologizes and hopes to return, the marriage partner may refuse to rec-oncile. He or she may not want to risk another shattered heart.

TRUE SACRIFICES

Hosea's message in chapter 14 echoes King David's words:

For You will not delight in sacrifice, or I would give it;
You will not be pleased with a burnt offering.
The sacrifices of God are a broken spirit;
a broken and contrite heart, O God, You will not despise.
(Psalm 51:16–17)

God's Old Testament covenant with His people established sacrifices and burnt offerings as outward, meaningful signs of a repentant heart. Throughout Hosea, we've read how the people of Israel still observed these traditions. But they did so without faith, without contrition. In their pagan mindset, they followed the rites as a way of manipulating God, thinking, *If I sacrifice this bull, God will overlook my adultery. Instead of curses, I'll receive blessings.*

But both Hosea's and David's words tell us that God desires honest contrition more than going through the motions of ritual. Like any wronged husband, He wants the unfaithful bride to demonstrate a heart broken in remorse so the relationship can begin to heal.

God didn't have to take Israel back after all of her unfaithfulness, but He does. In some of the most beautiful words in the whole Book of Hosea, Yahweh speaks:

I will heal their apostasy;
I will love them freely,
for My anger has turned from them.
I will be like the dew to Israel;
he shall blossom like the lily;
he shall take root like the trees of Lebanon;
his shoots shall spread out;
his beauty shall be like the olive,

and his fragrance like Lebanon.
They shall return and dwell beneath My shadow;
   they shall flourish like the grain;
they shall blossom like the vine;
   their fame shall be like the wine of Lebanon.
O Ephraim, what have I to do with idols?
   It is I who answer and look after you.
I am like an evergreen cypress;
   from Me comes your fruit. (Hosea 14:4–8)

This is no forced wedding. God promises to love His people *freely*.

"I will love them freely"—what delightful words! Not "I will love them reluctantly." Not "I will love them begrudgingly." Not "I will love them but resent every minute." God doesn't love them at arm's length. This is no forced wedding. God promises to love His people *freely*. Yahweh voluntarily bestows tenderness, affection, and devotion on His beloved.

LOVE

The Hebrew word for "love," *ahab*, is used more often in Hosea than in any other book of prophecy. In the mere fourteen chapters of Hosea, *ahab* appears thirteen times compared with nine appearances in the sixty-six chapters of Isaiah and ten in the fifty-two chapters of Jeremiah. Although Hosea's message contains words of warning and judgment, he also highlights God's constant love.

But before the relationship can be mended, God must "heal their apostasy" (v. 4). The people can't heal the broken bond by their own willpower. They can't quit backsliding by the strength of their own resolve. As wayward humans, we need God to give us the power to come back to Him. His love heals our rebellious ways and strengthens us to change.

Because of Yahweh's love, Israel will flourish. Their love story will continue. God paints a picture of the blessings His beloved will receive when they finally return. He will refresh their land and their hearts just like dew waters the land in the dry season. They will blossom like a lily—a lovely, delicate flower. God will keep them as firmly rooted in their land as the great trees of Lebanon stand rooted in that neighboring country. He will grant bountiful growth so they can spread out. Their scent and beauty will attract many.

Yahweh compares Himself to an evergreen cypress tree—a graceful tree that can grow to an enormous size.[77] He reminds them that He is the one who answers their desperate cries in the night, the one who tenderly watches over them and provides what they need.

God promises, "They shall return and dwell beneath My shadow" (v. 7). I love this image: when Israel finally comes back to Yahweh, He will draw them so close that they will rest in His shadow. A shadow provides shade from the hot sun; it offers a place to relax. Imagine sitting in God's shadow. Picture the peace and comfort you would experience in the presence of God's strength, protection, and care.

Ironically, Israel had attempted to find abundance on their own by worshiping Baal and Asherah, the pagan gods of fertility. But the pagan fertility rites led to spiritual sterility. If only they had trusted God wholeheartedly, they would have received the blessings He had already prepared.

Listen to God's words—they are for you too. He whispers to your heart:

> Stop striving to fit into the world and working hard to appease the false gods of affluence and materialism. They can never give you what your heart desires. Come to Me and I will love you freely. You don't have to twist My arm. You don't have to jump through hoops. Your empty heart hungers for love, but even greater than your desire to receive love is My desire to give it. Come close enough to sit in My shadow. Come near enough to know My protection, My care, and My affection. I will love you freely.

DEW IN ISRAEL

In Hosea 14, God promised, "I will be like the dew to Israel" (v. 5). In the land of Israel, plants rely on dew during the dry season. From April to October, very little rain falls, and plants need the morning dew for moisture. Just as the dew sustains plants, God's love nourishes our spiritually dry hearts.

And just as plants cannot water themselves, we can't produce faith or repentance on our own. Luther wrote in his explanation of the Apostles' Creed, "I believe that I cannot by my own reason or strength believe in Jesus Christ, my Lord, or come to Him; but the Holy Spirit has called me by the Gospel, enlightened me with His gifts, sanctified and kept me in the true faith."[78] God's love rains down, softening the soil of our hard hearts, and the Holy Spirit produces the fruit of faith.[79]

A HAPPY ENDING FOR ALL OF US

Because we know the history of Israel, we know that their happy ending didn't come during Hosea's lifetime. Hosea's fellow countrymen refused to listen to his warnings. King Hoshea of the Northern Kingdom tried to retain his rule by first paying off Assyria and then going to Egypt for help. But in the end, powerful Assyria invaded Israel, laid siege to the capital city of Samaria for three years, then shut Hoshea in prison and deported many Israelites to Assyria.

But Hosea's last recorded words do not dwell on the destruction of the nation. Instead, he looks ahead to a time when descendants of his countrymen will repent and return. A time when God will again love them freely and restore their intimate relationship.

Hosea tells all of us that his words apply to anyone who will listen:

> Whoever is wise, let him understand these things;
> whoever is discerning, let him know them;
> for the ways of the LORD are right,
> and the upright walk in them,
> but transgressors stumble in them. (Hosea 14:9)

143

Hosea calls out to the wise and discerning: "Pay attention—this message is for you." God instructed Hosea to live out a strange love story. This was no romantic comedy. In this bizarre plotline, Hosea married a woman who played the part of a prostitute. He knew of her tawdry reputation. He probably suspected she would be unfaithful. Yet in obedience to God, he took her as his wife. The vivid names of their children told the message the prophet tried to give his neighbors. Jezreel's name spoke of the judgment against the wicked kings of Israel. No Mercy's birth brought the news that God's leniency and patience would soon end. God named Hosea's third child Not My People to tell the people of Israel, "You are not My people, and I am not your God" (1:9).

Unfortunately, Hosea's suspicions came true: Gomer did not stay faithful to Hosea. Her betrayal probably stabbed Hosea's heart like a knife, yet God said, "Go again, love a woman who is loved by another man and is an adulteress, even as the LORD loves the children of Israel, though they turn to other gods and love cakes of raisins" (3:1). Because Gomer walked into some kind of trouble, Hosea had to buy her back with the equivalent of thirty shekels of silver—the price of a slave. While other men bought Gomer to use her, Hosea bought her to save her. In spite of her unfaithfulness, he redeemed her, loved her, and told her, "You are mine and I am yours."

God chose to use Hosea's extraordinary love story as a real-life portrayal of His own love affair with Israel. He chose the descendants of Abraham as His very own. He promised His love and protection as long as they faithfully loved and trusted Him. But as omniscient God, He knew what would happen. While Hosea probably suspected Gomer's future infidelity, God knew without a doubt that His beloved Israel would give her heart to other lovers, other gods. Even then, God continued to love His people. He sought them out, although they blatantly dishonored the marriage relationship by having affairs with Baal and Asheroth and courting favors with Assyria and Egypt. All the while they were acting out their two-timing ways, He patiently called out to them to return.

But when they didn't return, God disciplined them by allowing foreign powers to defeat and destroy. After the destruction of the Northern Kingdom, nearly two hundred years would pass before some of the children of Israel would return to their homeland and renew their relationship with Yahweh.

Just as Hosea looked forward to the time when Israel would again live as God's bride, the prophet Isaiah also wrote of the marriage relationship between the Lord's chosen people and Yahweh. He wrote:

> You shall no more be termed Forsaken,
>   and your land shall no more be termed Desolate,
> but you shall be called My Delight Is in Her,
>   and your land Married;
> for the LORD delights in you,
>   and your land shall be married.
> For as a young man marries a young woman,
>   so shall your sons marry you,
> and as the bridegroom rejoices over the bride,
>   so shall your God rejoice over you. . . .
> And they shall be called The Holy People,
>   The Redeemed of the LORD;
> and you shall be called Sought Out,
>   A City Not Forsaken. (Isaiah 62:4–5, 12)

God's loving nature means He will never forsake His people. And when they return, they will have a whole new set of names. Instead of Jezreel, No Mercy, and Not My People, God calls them *My Delight Is in Her*, *Married*, *The Holy People*, *The Redeemed of the Lord*. He gives them the name *Sought Out*, for He has never stopped seeking them, never stopped hoping for renewal of their marriage relationship.

THE BRIDE OF CHRIST

God's love story doesn't end with the return of Israel to the Promised Land. Seven hundred years after Hosea, Jesus came into the world to redeem His Bride, the Church. He knew of her unfaithfulness; He knew she would often let Him down. And yet the Prince of Peace came, seeking His beloved. Because she had also stepped into trouble, racking up a debt of sin and shame, He needed to buy her back with the price of His own life.

Jesus loved us freely. He willingly paid the price so we could be His own. Because of Christ, we can all have a better-than-fairy-tale ending. The Prince comes into our lives and asks us to say yes to His never-ending love and grace.

We may find it hard to believe because we've often acted like Gomer, looking for love in all the wrong places, seeking acceptance in the eyes of the world. Perhaps we've spent more time with other lovers like career and entertainment than with Jesus. Maybe we've looked to accomplishment, wealth, and material goods to satisfy us instead of God.

Yet, just as Hosea searched for Gomer, Jesus looks for you. He gives you the name *Sought Out* because He has never stopped pursuing your heart. And just like Hosea bought back Gomer, Jesus redeemed you with His own blood so you can bear the name *The Redeemed of the Lord*.

Now we wait for the marriage ceremony. The apostle John writes of this grand wedding in Revelation:

> Then I heard what seemed to be the voice of a great multitude, like the roar of many waters and like the sound of mighty peals of thunder, crying out,
> "Hallelujah!
> For the Lord our God
>   the Almighty reigns.
> Let us rejoice and exult
>   and give Him the glory,
> for the marriage of the Lamb has come,

> and His Bride has made herself ready;
> it was granted her to clothe herself
> with fine linen, bright and pure"—
> for the fine linen is the righteous deeds of the saints.
> And the angel said to me, "Write this: Blessed are those who
> are invited to the marriage supper of the Lamb." And he said
> to me, "These are the true words of God." (Revelation 19:6–9)

Through Baptism and the gift of faith, we have been betrothed to Christ, but in heaven, we will experience the wedding—the fullness of our marriage to our Redeemer, Savior, Prince.

Remember the names He calls you—My Delight Is in You, Married, The Redeemed of the Lord, and Sought Out.

Although our puny minds can't fathom the glory of heaven, take a moment to read those verses from Revelation again. Put yourself in the scene as the bride. Picture yourself clothed in Christ's righteousness (see Isaiah 61:10)—a dress in the whitest of whites. Imagine the face of Jesus, and remember the names He calls you—My Delight Is in You, Married, The Redeemed of the Lord, and Sought Out. Bask in the relentless love of your Redeemer, Pursuer, Husband.

LIVE LIKE YOU'RE LOVED

We may need to wait for the marriage ceremony, but we can still live in the relentless love of the One who comes to us and calls us His Bride.

Satan, of course, doesn't want us to see God as our lover. He wants us to look at God as the rule-giver, stern-judger, and fun-spoiler. He wants you to picture Him only as an angry deity. He hopes you will regard Him as a harsh taskmaster. Satan works overtime to present this view of God because if he succeeds, religion becomes a duty. Faith becomes a list of dos and don'ts. Relationship with God turns into a taxing obligation.

JEWISH WEDDINGS

A Jewish marriage began with a betrothal, an agreement between the families of the bride and groom. This betrothal was somewhat like our modern engagements, but betrothals were considered as legally binding as marriage.

About a year after the betrothal, the bride and groom celebrated their union with a formal ceremony. On the day of the wedding, the bride would bathe and purify herself, then dress in her most beautiful clothing and jewels. In the evening, the groom would come to her house and lead her and her friends and family through the streets to the home he had prepared for her. After the couple signed the marriage covenant, everyone would enjoy a lavish feast.[80]

But the Book of Hosea demonstrates that God wants so much more. He wants you to see Him as your lover, your husband, your confidant. Jesus wants you to know Him intimately, even as He knows every little thing about you. He doesn't want you to run away, but if you do, He won't stop pursuing you. He desires your faithfulness, not because He wants to be your boss but because He wants to be your husband. He wants your relationship with Him to be a passionate love affair.

Each of us can experience this intimacy with Jesus. Whether you're in a loving earthly marriage, a marriage that has disappointed, or no marriage at all, you can know the relentless love of Jesus. You can have the mind-boggling experience of knowing your Savior intimately and of being known.

This changes everything. Spending time in the Bible becomes an opportunity to discover something new about our Husband and hear His declarations of love. Prayer becomes a chance to reciprocate that love. Because of the certainty of His affection, we know we can unburden our hearts and tell Him our secret fears. We no longer need to strive for recognition or compete for accolades because we live confident in the love of the King. We can drop our masks, assured that Jesus loves us for who we are and not for who the world thinks we should be. And worship becomes a time to receive that love in the celebration that is the Lord's Supper and to praise our Husband for His sure and unconditional love for us.

We can drop our masks, assured that Jesus loves us for who we are and not for who the world thinks we should be.

Listen to the Lord's words: "I will love them freely" (Hosea 14:4). Jesus' love knows no bounds. Live in the relentless love of Christ.

Epilogue

Love and loss and love again. We've seen this plotline throughout the Book of Hosea.

I began this book with my own broken love story with my now-husband, John. A cute guy preparing to serve God as a pastor sought out a small-town girl. The relationship began well with dates at local movie theaters and picnics in parks. But then I got scared. Not ready for a serious relationship, I went off looking for more excitement. After I finished the year of touring the country with a musical group, John came back into my life—even after I had rejected him. His forgiveness and acceptance re-started our relationship that has now lasted decades.

My relationship with John had an unusual beginning, but Hosea and Gomer's relationship had an even stranger start. God instructed preacher and prophet Hosea to marry a prostitute. Hosea sought out Gomer and married her. But even after three children, Gomer wasn't ready to get "serious." She left the marriage—perhaps in search of more excitement. God instructed Hosea to find Gomer, pay her debts, and love her again.

God used Hosea and Gomer's unique love story to illustrate His own commitment to His chosen nation, Israel. Yahweh didn't choose Israel because of its greatness. The nation started out like a small-town girl in a neighborhood of strong, influential people. But God made this ragtag group of former slaves into a powerful and prosperous nation. Unfortunately, Israel also didn't want to be tied down to one love, and she sought out other lovers like Baal and Asheroth and looked to other sources like Egypt and Assyria to meet her needs. God could have given up on the relationship, but throughout the Book of Hosea, we see His constant pursuit of Israel's heart—and His anticipation of the day when she would repent and return to Him.

All these accounts mirror the greatest love story of all. The Father created us to live in intimate relationship with Him, but ever since the incident of eating forbidden fruit in a perfect garden, we fickle humans have gone off looking for something more. We haven't been faithful to the one true God. We've loved houses and health more than Jesus. We've worshiped success and security. We've bowed to money and materialism.

God could have given up on us, but He loved us too much to let us go. So He sent His Son to pay our debt of sin—to buy us back with His own life so we could live with Him forever. Jesus' sacrifice gives us the ultimate happy ending to the greatest love story of all time.

But even when we have experienced God's love, we may—like Gomer—wander away from that love. Our hearts may doubt His affection when financial struggles or health problems arrive in our lives. Our not-so-pristine pasts might haunt our minds with suggestions that Jesus could never love us after what we've done. So we go looking for attention and affirmation from other sources.

The extraordinary account of faithful Hosea and his wayward wife helps us glimpse God's passionate love for us. This ancient tale helps us see how much He desires us to know Him intimately. The story of Gomer tells us that even though we may have drifted away from God's love or doubted His devotion, God's tender voice continues to call us chosen. Treasured. Loved.

I pray that your time in the Book of Hosea will help these truths sink deep into your soul. That the pondering of the account of prophet and prostitute will help you live transformed by the unwavering love of God. When you're convinced no one could love you as you are, remember the price Christ paid for you. When you're tempted to strive to become more significant, recall your great worth in Jesus' eyes.

Live forever changed by the relentless love of God.

STUDY GUIDE

Go deeper into Hosea by delving into the pages of his book and contemplating the lessons he taught. The study questions that follow will help you discover God's relentless love in the ancient story of a faithful prophet and his wayward wife. I have organized the questions in levels—not levels of difficulty, but levels of time.

Level 1: Reflect on the Reading. If you have only fifteen minutes, complete this section. These questions will help you reflect on the chapter's lessons and make them more personal. And if you are doing the study in a group, these questions will start conversation flowing.

Level 2: Dig into the Word. If you have more time, dive deeper into the Word by reading the relevant section of Hosea and answering questions designed to help you understand this book of prophecy.

Level 3: Apply the Word to Your Life. These activities will give you ways to personalize Hosea's message to your faith walk.

Level 4: Create a Project. To help you internalize what you have learned, I have provided some practical exercises and hands-on activities. To encourage your heart, I've also included a playlist of music. You can find recordings of these songs on YouTube or on a streaming service like Spotify. If you are doing this study in a group, consider doing the activities together as people arrive for the study. The suggested songs could be playing in the background to create an atmosphere conducive to remembering God's relentless love. Perhaps one member of the group could take charge of getting materials for these projects and another could be responsible for obtaining the playlist for the session.

To get the most out of this study, I encourage you to complete all the levels. But life is hectic—do what you can!

CHAPTER ONE:

GOD'S RELENTLESS LOVE CALLS YOU HIS OWN

Study Questions

REFLECT ON THE READING

1. Do you have a story of rejection and reconciliation? With your spouse? relative? friend? How were you able to reconcile?

2. Imagine yourself in Hosea's sandals. How might you respond to God's instruction to marry a person known for infidelity? (Remember: God does not ask the same of us, but cautions us to marry a godly spouse.)

3. If you had lived during Hosea's time, how would you have reacted when hearing the names of the prophet's children?

4. What is your biggest takeaway from this chapter?

DIG INTO THE WORD

1. The Book of Hosea has many contrasts: contrasts of judgment and love, Law and Gospel.

   a. Read Hosea 1:1–2:1. In the table below, write the contrasts of Law and Gospel.

Harsh Words (Law)	Loving Words (Gospel)
Hosea 1:4–5 House of Jehu will be punished End of kingdom of Israel breaking bow of Israel	Hosea 1:11 Children of Israel + Judah Reunite + shall appoint one head
Hosea 1:6 No mercy on Israel No forgiveness	Hosea 2:1 you are my people + receive mercy
Hosea 1:9 Not my people I won't be your God	Hosea 1:10, 2:1 Children of the Living God God says you are my people

   b. Now discover contrasts of Law and Gospel in the New Testament.

Words of Law	Words of Gospel
Romans 3:23 Everyone has sinned + fallen short of Glory of God	Romans 3:24–25 Justified by Grace through Redemption that is Jesus Christ. shows God's righteousness
Ephesians 2:1–2 Dead in trespasses + sins.	Ephesians 2:8–9 saved through Faith saved by Grace through faith
Colossians 2:13a Dead in trespasses + sins	Colossians 2:13b–14 God made alive together c̄ him having forgiven us all our trespasses.

(Ten Commandments)

c. The Law speaks of God's requirements. Read Romans 7:7. Why do we need words of Law?

Shows us our sins ("SOS" = show our sins – as Luther says.

d. The Gospel speaks God's Good News of salvation through Jesus. Read Romans 3:20–22. Why do we need words of Gospel? *To know forgiveness from God we can be saved through salvation/faith.*

e. Talk about the effects of Law and Gospel in your own life.

APPLY THE WORD TO YOUR LIFE

In the first chapter of Hosea, we read about God's reversals.

1. At first, He told the people of Israel, "You are not My people, and I am not your God" (Hosea 1:9).

    a. Imagine how you might have felt as an Israelite in Hosea's day when you heard those words.
    possibly deep sorrow

b. What might your life look like if you didn't know God?

2. Thankfully, God relented and spoke mercy. Read Hosea 1:10 and Romans 9:22–26.

   a. Compare Hosea 1:10 with Romans 9:26. What do you notice?

   Romans is quoting Hosea

   b. In Romans 9:24, to whom does Paul say this passage applies?

   Applies to not only Jews but Gentiles

   c. Personalize Romans 9:25–26 by writing your name in the blanks:

   "Those who were not My people I will call 'My people,'
   and _____ *I* _____ who was not beloved I will call
   'beloved.'"
   "And in the very place where it was said to them, 'You are not
   My people,'
   there _____ *I* _____ will be called '[child] of the
   living God.'"

d. Describe the advantages of being in a family.

Cared for, loved, protected, support

e. Apply these advantages to being a child of God.

See above
God never disappoints

f. Write a prayer thanking God for calling you His own.

CREATE A PROJECT

1. After God speaks words of judgment, He relents and speaks words of love. He redeems the names He gave Hosea's children. Without Christ, we bear the names *Lost*, *Sinner*, and *Condemned*. But in our Baptism, He places His name upon us. Because of Jesus, He gives us new names.

    a. Look up the following passages, and match each passage with the name God gives us.

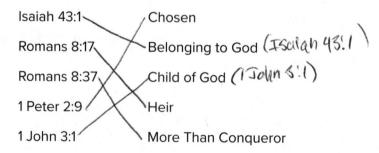

Isaiah 43:1   Chosen

Romans 8:17   Belonging to God *(Isaiah 43:1)*

Romans 8:37   Child of God *(1 John 3:1)*

1 Peter 2:9   Heir

1 John 3:1   More Than Conqueror

b. Which of these names means the most to you today? Why is it meaningful?

c. Consider making an artistic rendering of the verse associated with that name. Use art pens and colored pencils or your computer's fancy fonts. Post your creation where you will see it often this week.

d. If you are doing this study with a group, consider beginning your session with everyone writing their favorite name on a name tag and explaining what that name means to them.

2. Praise God for His relentless love in song. Listen to "You Say" by Lauren Daigle, "Love Came Down" by Kari Jobe, or "Live Like You're Loved" by Hawk Nelson. Or sing a hymn like "Go, My Children, with My Blessing" (*LSB* 922) or "The Love of God."[81]

CHAPTER TWO:
GOD'S RELENTLESS LOVE PURSUES

Study Questions

REFLECT ON THE READING

1. Steven brought diet cola to Theresa every day to win her over. If someone you didn't particularly like wanted to build a relationship with you, what should he or she bring? Caramel lattes? Dark chocolate?

2. Think of the two meanings of *court* in this chapter. How did God *court* Israel in these two ways?

3. How has God *courted* you?

4. What is your biggest takeaway from this chapter?
   God doesn't give up on us

DIG INTO THE WORD

1. Hosea 2:20 says, "I will betroth you to Me in faithfulness. And you shall *know* the LORD" (emphasis added). God longs for us to know Him intimately. Read Hosea 2, and let this chapter help you know Yahweh better. As you read, take note of what you learn about God. I have done the first two verses for you.

    a. Hosea 2:2–3 God is hurt when I am unfaithful.

    b. Hosea 2:8–9 God wants me to know that His gifts of food and other material goods are signs of His love.

    c. Hosea 2:14 – seek us out, uses wilderness times to draw me closer

    d. Hosea 2:16 - God wants us to love a loving relationship; not one who with one who controls us (a relationship)

    e. Hosea 2:19 God loves me forever

    pg204

    f. Hosea 2:20 - God wants me to truly know him.

    pg 204

2. Which characteristic of Yahweh means most to you right now? Why is that one significant?

Pg 204,

APPLY THE WORD TO YOUR LIFE

Hosea 2 may expand our view of God and challenge us to examine subconscious beliefs about God that we have held for a long time.

1. Use the following prompts to journal about your views of God.

    a. Hosea 2:16 reminds us, "And in that day, declares the LORD, you will call Me 'My Husband,' and no longer will you call Me 'My Baal.'" Remember that the Hebrew word for "husband," *'iysh*, refers to a man, husband, or marriage partner. The second, *Ba'ally*, brings more of the meaning of "lord," "master," and the legal rights of a husband over a wife.

    Do I view God as a master who issues rules to obey—someone I need to impress with my obedience and hard work? Or do I think of Him as someone who loves me intimately?

    There's a difference in relationship btw husband + one c the Lord.
    Gift from God because he loves us
    vs. Doing things to please God to receive "gifts"

    b. Hosea 2:14a says, "Therefore, behold, I will allure her, and bring her into the wilderness."

How do I regard wilderness times? Do I see them only as punishment? Or do I consider them opportunities to draw closer to the One who loves me?

c. Hosea 2:14b tells us that God speaks tenderly to His beloved.

Do I look at God's Word as my Lover's tender expressions? Do I spend time in the Word to know the One who longs to care for my soul and reassure me of His love? Or do I tend to view my Bible reading as a tedious duty or academic pursuit?

2. How has the story of Hosea and Gomer, Yahweh and Israel, changed your view of God? – Reinforces that God loves us unconditionally.

3. Write a prayer praising God for who He is, using what you have learned about Him in Hosea 2.

CREATE A PROJECT

1. In Hosea 2:16, God looks forward to the day when Israel will call Him "My Husband." Jesus compared Himself to a bridegroom (see Matthew 9:14–15), and Paul compared a husband-wife relationship to Christ's relationship with the Church (see Ephesians 5:25–27). Scripture often speaks of our relationship with God in terms of marriage.

   This week, dig out some of your wedding photos or pull up the pictures of a recent marriage ceremony you attended. Think about the ceremony with its promises of faithfulness and commitment. Remember the expressions on the faces of the bride and groom at the wedding you attended or your own emotions on your big day. Now compare those to your relationship with God. What is alike? What is different? (Consider sharing the photos you found at your group meeting.)

2. Praise God for His relentless love in song. Listen to "Prince Song" by 2nd Chapter of Acts or "Love Moved First" by Casting Crowns. Or sing a hymn like "Jesus, Your Boundless Love So True" (*LW* 280) or "My Song Is Love Unknown" (*LSB* 430).

CHAPTER THREE:
GOD'S RELENTLESS LOVE REDEEMS

Study Questions

REFLECT ON THE READING

1. Dick and Mary have celebrated their sixty-eighth wedding anniversary! Mary's advice for a long and happy marriage was "Trust each other," and Dick advised, "Bend a little." Do you agree with their suggestions? Why or why not?

2. What relationship advice can you share? What do you do to get along with others? Give + take

3. God told Hosea, "Go again, love a woman who is loved by another man and is an adulteress" (Hosea 3:1). If God gave you the instruction to love a person who had hurt you and abandoned you, what would your reaction be? It would be difficult but God wants us to love others.

4. What is your biggest takeaway from this chapter?

1. Read Hosea 3. Then read the following passages:

Jeremiah 29:13

Romans 5:8

Deuteronomy 6:13–14

Isaiah 43:1

Titus 2:11–14

Fill out the following chart, using these steps (I have done the first one for you):

- Match each verse from Hosea with a related verse from the list above.
- Write the shared theme of the verses. What do both verses talk about?
- What truth can you take from those verses for your life today?

Verse from Hosea	Related Verse	Theme of the Verses	Truth for Today
Hosea 3:1	Romans 5:8	Gomer didn't deserve Hosea's love. We don't deserve God's love.	Our feelings of shame and guilt can keep us from receiving God's love. The good news is that we can all have God's love because of His grace. We don't have to work for it or pretty ourselves up in order to deserve it.

Verse from Hosea	Related Verse	Theme of the Verses	Truth for Today
Hosea 3:2	Is Titus 2:11-14 ?, Isaiah 43-1	Redemption- Hosea Redeemed Gomer.	Jesus gave himself to redeem us. us Truth for today -Live upright That's how much we mean to Him.
Hosea 3:3	Deuteronomy 6:13-14 2 Romans Isiah,	we belong We belong to God.	every culture.
Hosea 3:4	Deut. 6:13-14	We belong to God	
Hosea 3:5	Jer. 29:13	Seek the Lord	

see pg 205

APPLY THE WORD TO YOUR LIFE

In chapter 3, we explored Gomer's possible emotions when Hosea needed to buy her back and how her feelings might mirror some of our own. Take a minute to reflect on these feelings and how they can draw us to God.

1. How do you think Gomer felt when Hosea bought her back for the price of a slave? (Circle any you think she experienced.)

could be several different feelings

✓ Grateful   Shamed   Joyful

Guilty   Valued   ✓ Devalued

Loved   Embarrassed   Inferior

could be similar to Prodigal Son.
Why do you think she felt those emotions?

2. What is your primary emotion when you realize that Jesus redeemed you with the highest price possible? (Choose from the emotions listed in question 1 or choose your own.)
Grateful, Loved, Valued, Joyful, I may feel guilty of my sins.
Why that emotion?

3. Do you think Gomer deserved to be rescued? Why or why not?

4. Read 2 Timothy 1:8–10.

   a. Do we deserve to be rescued from sin and death (v. 9)?

   No.

   b. How can we receive God's redeeming love and grace (vv. 9–10)? *He saved us through faith; through Jesus Christ*

5. Have you ever struggled to accept the fact of God's relentless love for you, even though you believe in Christ's death for you? (If you want, give details of that struggle.) *Comforting to know about His relentless love. God/Jesus has forgiven/forgotten my sins.*

   We have an advocate in Jesus before the Father

   How does Gomer's story help you draw closer to God and His relentless love?

God's Relentless Love

CREATE A PROJECT

1. Hosea and Gomer's marriage became a real-life analogy of God's bond with His people. But Hosea is not the only book in the Bible that uses marriage as an illustration of our relationship with the Lord. One commentary states, "The purpose of all marriage sign-acts, metaphors, and imagery throughout the Scriptures is to proclaim Jesus Christ."[82] It also asserts, "Each of us is intended to perceive in Hosea's marriage a divine message of mercy and great reversals that is also for us!"[83]

   a. Look up the following verses and write down what you learn about your relationship with God.

   Ephesians 5:25–27
   Describes how Christ loves the church.

   2 Corinthians 11:2

   Isaiah 54:5 *(see pg 171.*

   Isaiah 62:5 *God rejoices over us.*

170

b. Create an artistic project based on one of these verses. Consider making a collage with materials commonly used at weddings: white satin, lace, tulle, rice, flowers, rings. (If you are doing the study in a group, have one person make a trip to a craft store to pick up these items.) Paste these on a piece of cardstock or poster board and then put your chosen verse in the center of the collage. I have made a little printable of Isaiah 54:5 for you to use, if you wish. Photocopy this printable, cut it out, and use it in your collage. Post your collage in a prominent place to remind you of the relentless love God has for you.

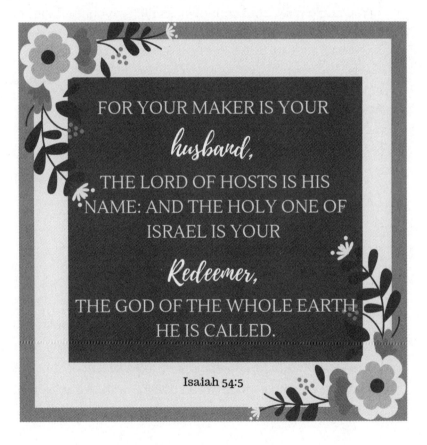

FOR YOUR MAKER IS YOUR

husband,

THE LORD OF HOSTS IS HIS NAME: AND THE HOLY ONE OF ISRAEL IS YOUR

Redeemer,

THE GOD OF THE WHOLE EARTH HE IS CALLED.

Isaiah 54:5

2. Praise God for His relentless love in song. Listen to "Wanted" by Danny Gokey or "The God Who Stays" by Matthew West. Or sing a hymn like "O Bride of Christ, Rejoice" (*LSB* 335) or "Chief of Sinners Though I Be" (*LSB* 611).

CHAPTER FOUR:

GOD'S RELENTLESS LOVE RESTORES

Study Questions

REFLECT ON THE READING

1. I admire Scott's relentless love for Logan. His comment "As a parent, anyone will do whatever they need to for their child" is usually true, but his exemplary commitment far exceeds what I consider ordinary. When have you seen or experienced parental sacrifice? (You could talk about your own sacrifices, your parents' sacrifices, or the acts of other parents.)

2. Compare and contrast a caring parent's love for his or her child with the relentless love God has for each of us. How are the two alike? How are they different?

    alike — both unconditional
    different — God is perfect

3. In this section of Hosea, we looked at how the Israelites turned to foreign powers for help instead of almighty God. When are you most tempted to turn to worldly sources of help instead of God—when faced with a crisis? when dealing with everyday problems? Why?

4. What is your biggest takeaway from this chapter?

Return to God

DIG INTO THE WORD

1. Read Hosea 4–7. Use the chart below to record each chapter's key idea. Then write down a lesson God wants Israel to learn and a lesson you can apply to your life today. Each chapter contains many ideas and lessons, so your answers may differ from others in your group.

Chapter	Key Idea	God's Lesson for Israel	A Lesson for My Life
Hosea 4 ⊘ faithfulness in Israel → ⊘ steadfast love Hesid → Love in Hebrew		Famine? Beasts as sacrifices punishment	Don't lose knowledge of God 4:6 – Important
Hosea 5 God charges Israel + issues punishment Priest Israel the king	punishment until earnestly seek him prodigal son can't hide from God	defeated by the Assyrians ★ Don't rely on worldly sources (eg self-help)	tough love prodigal son turn to God
Hosea 6 Israel & Judah are unrepentant 6:2 points us toward Christ + Easter	Return to God to restore – wants us to return	Return to God who longs to restore us Israel restoration	Hosea 6:6 Know God personally + intimately
Hosea 7 Evidence of Israel sins Israel turn to wrong sources for healing they turn to many kings. People	God longs for Israel to repent. But they turn to other nations	Return upward Ho 7:16	Hosea 7:1 + 16

of Israel are turning
to manmade sources
for strength instead
of God

2. In the last column, circle the most crucial lesson for your life today, and answer the following questions.

   a. Why is that lesson important for your life now?

   b. Name one specific action you could take to apply that lesson to your life this week.

APPLY THE WORD TO YOUR LIFE

Hosea 4–7 emphasized the important theme of the knowledge of God. The prophet called out to the people, "Let us know; let us press on to know the LORD" (Hosea 6:3). Hosea was not the only author in the Bible who made knowledge of God a priority in his writings. Find Philippians 3:8 in the Bible and read about the apostle Paul's passion for knowing God.

1. Write out the verse from your favorite translation of Scripture.

2. I love the way the Amplified Bible, Classic Edition expresses this verse:

Yes, furthermore, I count everything as loss compared to the possession of the priceless privilege (the overwhelming preciousness, the surpassing worth, and supreme advantage) of knowing Christ Jesus my Lord *and* of progressively becoming more deeply *and* intimately acquainted with Him [of perceiving and recognizing and understanding Him more fully and clearly]. For His sake I have lost everything and consider it all to be mere rubbish (refuse, dregs), in order that I may win (gain) Christ (the Anointed One). (Philippians 3:8 AMPC)

How does this version expand your understanding of the word *knowing*?

3. Let's explore the meaning of the word *know* even more. Below, I have supplied the meaning of the Hebrew word translated as "know" in Hosea 6:3 and the Greek word used for "knowing" in Philippians 3:8. Now you supply the meaning for the English word *know* by looking it up in a dictionary or thesaurus.

- Hebrew word *yada*: "to know by perceiving, to know by experience, to know carnally"

- Greek word *gnosis*: "knowledge, understanding, moral wisdom"

- English word *know*:

4. Considering all you have gleaned from these definitions and what you have learned from Hosea and Paul about knowing God, write what it now means to you to know Christ.

5. List some practical ways we can become more intimately acquainted with the Lord (e.g., make a list of the characteristics of God). Circle one activity to practice this week.

CREATE A PROJECT

1. Hosea uses the binding up of wounds as a beautiful word picture of God's restoration. First, God chides Israel and Judah for going to Assyria for healing—which earthly kings could not give (see Hosea 5:13). Then He reminds them that He tears only so He may heal (see 6:1), and finally, He promises restoration and healing in the future (see 6:11–7:1).

   To remind yourself of God's desire to heal your sin-stained soul and restore you to spiritual health, consider wearing a bandage today with the words "He will bind us up" (Hosea 6:1). Write the words on a bandage with permanent marker and then put it on your hand or arm where you will see it often today. Use it as a reminder to look to God for healing and restoration rather than to ineffective, worldly sources.

2. Praise God for His relentless love in song. Listen to "What Love Is This" by Kari Jobe or "The More I Seek You" by Gateway Worship. Or sing a hymn like "Jesus, Lover of My Soul" (*LW* 508) or "A Mighty Fortress Is Our God" (*LSB* 657).

CHAPTER FIVE:

GOD'S RELENTLESS LOVE RAINS RIGHTEOUSNESS

Study Questions

REFLECT ON THE READING

1. When have your relationship choices ended badly? Have you pursued a romantic relationship with someone who later demonstrated unfaithfulness? Have you had a friendship with someone who turned out to be untrustworthy?

2. Martin Luther wrote: "A god means that from which we are to expect all good and in which we are to take refuge in all distress. . . . I say that whatever you set your heart on and put your trust in is truly your God."[84] Write this important truth in your own words.

3. Does picturing God as a brokenhearted husband change the way you view the Book of Hosea? Or does it change the way you view your relationship with the Lord? Explain.

4. What is your biggest takeaway from this chapter?

DIG INTO THE WORD

1. Read Hosea 8–10. Use the chart below to record each chapter's key idea. Then write a lesson God wants Israel to learn and a lesson you can apply to your life today. Each chapter contains many ideas and lessons, so your answers may differ from others in your group.

Chapter	Key Idea	God's Lesson for Israel	A Lesson for My Life
Hosea 8			
Hosea 9			
Hosea 10			

2. In the last column, circle the most crucial lesson for your life today and answer the following questions.

    a. Why is that lesson important for your life now?

    b. Name one specific action you could take to apply that lesson to your life this week.

APPLY THE WORD TO YOUR LIFE

Hosea 8–10 focused on the counterfeit gods the Israelites worshiped—the false loves they clung to. Our modern idols may not look like carved statues, yet we all have a tendency to worship false gods. Let's use the three-step process we explored in this chapter to identify our idols, repent of our false loves, and receive Christ's forgiveness.

Recognize. Prayerfully ask God to reveal any idols taking up space on the altar of your heart. Review the questions based on the activities of the ancient Israelites on pages 95 and 96. As you read, circle three or four that apply to your life right now. Next, write the most pertinent questions below, along with your answers. Recognize the counterfeit gods you worship. For instance, the question "What would you mourn for if you lost it?" revealed the fact that I had placed the blessing of family above my love for God.

1. Question:

   Answer:

2. Question:

   Answer:

3. Question:

   Answer:

Repent. A key theme in the Book of Hosea is "return." When we repent, we make a 180-degree turn back to God. We admit our sin and ask Him to remove the idol from our hearts. Write a prayer asking God to forgive the times you have given your love to imitation gods.

My prayer:

Receive. Receive God's forgiveness and the gentle rain of His righteousness. Look up the following verses and choose one to turn into a prayer of thanksgiving for Christ's atonement of your sins.

Psalm 103:10–14

Hebrews 8:12

1 John 1:9

My prayer:

CREATE A PROJECT

1. Of the false gods you identified above, choose the one your heart clings to most. Think of a practical step you could take to smash this idol. For instance, if you recognize that new, fashionable clothing and the need to always look your best has become an idol, you could institute a shopping fast. During the next week, stay out of stores and off internet shopping sites except for buying essentials like food and medicine. Then, after you have completed your practical step, record how this action helped eliminate the counterfeit god from your life.

   Idol:

   Practical step to smash it:

How this action helped:

2. Praise God for His relentless love in song. Listen to "Jesus Loves Me" by Chris Tomlin or "Like You Love Me" by Tauren Wells. Or sing a hymn like "O Love, How Deep" (*LSB* 544) or "When I Survey the Wondrous Cross" (*LSB* 425).

CHAPTER SIX:

GOD'S RELENTLESS LOVE NEVER GIVES UP

Study Questions

REFLECT ON THE READING

1. Have you witnessed a long, loving marriage? Or have you observed someone who loved relentlessly, even when the other person couldn't return that love? What words describe that kind of love?

2. If God knew that humans would disobey and reject Him, why did He create us? How does this expand or change your view of God?

3. In this chapter, we read, "God will never just move on and look for someone else. He never gives up on us. Even when we forget Him. Even when we worship counterfeit gods. Even when we chase other loves. Even when we are helpless. He will continually reach out in love, hoping we will trust in the mercy and grace He extends to us because of Jesus." Do these words comfort you? Do they bring hope to you for a loved one not currently responding to God's grace? Explain.

4. What is your biggest takeaway from this chapter?

DIG INTO THE WORD

Read Hosea 11. As you read, pay attention to the word pictures Hosea uses, then answer the questions below.

1. How does the prophet describe Israel's unfaithfulness?

2. How does Hosea give us a glimpse of God's heart?

3. In Hosea 11:9, Yahweh declares, "I am God and not a man." In this chapter, how does God describe Himself in human terms yet also show He is uniquely God?

APPLY THE WORD TO YOUR LIFE

Hosea often uses the imagery of marriage to describe God's love for His people. But chapter 11 uses other analogies to help us understand this relentless love: the tender love of a father, the compassion of an animal caretaker, the mercy of a judge, and the powerful love expressed in the roar of a lion. These images of God appear in other parts of Scripture too. What can we learn about God's love in these passages?

1. Choose the analogy that most speaks to your heart. Look up the references for that analogy. Write what you discover about God's love as you view it through that lens.

   The Tender Love of a Father

   Psalm 103:13

   Luke 15:11–32

   1 John 3:1

   The Compassion of an Animal Caretaker

   Psalm 23

   Matthew 11:28–30

   John 10:7–15

   The Mercy of a Judge

   Micah 7:18–19

   John 5:21–27

Romans 8:1–2

The Roar of a Lion

Hosea 5:14

Joel 3:16

Revelation 5:5–6

2. Explain how your understanding of God's love changed by viewing it through that particular lens.

CREATE A PROJECT

1. Consider making an easy leather wrap bracelet to remind yourself that God continually leads you with cords of kindness and bands of love, as Hosea 11:4 says. This project could be especially fun if you're doing the study with a group!

Leather Wrap Bracelet

Materials

- 13 inches of 5mm round leather cord

- 5–7 beads with 5mm holes (you might want to choose red beads or beads with a heart design to signify God's love)

- 5mm endcap clasp set

- Jewelry glue

Directions

String the beads onto the leather cord. Space them evenly. Use the jewelry glue to glue the end caps onto each end of the cord. The bracelet is designed to wrap around your wrist twice.[85]

2. Praise God for His relentless love in song. Listen to "Reckless Love" by Cory Asbury or "Good, Good Father" by Chris Tomlin. Or sing a hymn like "The King of Love My Shepherd Is" (*LSB* 709) or "What Wondrous Love Is This" (*LSB* 543).

CHAPTER SEVEN:

GOD'S RELENTLESS LOVE DISCIPLINES

Study Questions

REFLECT ON THE READING

1. Think about a time when you needed to discipline or correct someone. Did you have to punish your child? correct someone who made a mistake at work? Describe your feelings when you administered the discipline.

2. In this chapter, we read that even when God disciplines, He does it out of His relentless love. How can discipline be an act of love?

3. Is all discipline punitive? Can you think of examples of people in the Bible who didn't deserve punishment and yet experienced hardship?

4. What is your biggest takeaway from this chapter?

DIG INTO THE WORD

1. Read Hosea 12 and 13. This section of Hosea contains harsh words. Below, write some of the punishments God would send to the nation of Israel. I've done the first one for you.

   a. Hosea 12:14

   God would leave his bloodguilt on him, and repay him according to his disgraceful deeds.

   b. Hosea 13:3

   c. Hosea 13:7–8

   d. Hosea 13:15

   e. Hosea 13:16

2. Even though this passage leans heavily on the Law, it still contains some words of grace. What encouragement does God give?

 a. Hosea 12:6

 b. Hosea 13:4–5

 c. Hosea 13:14

APPLY THE WORD TO YOUR LIFE

1. This section of Hosea demonstrates the danger of undisciplined affluence. Read Hosea 12:8 and 13:6, and then circle the following things that happened when the nation of Israel experienced prosperity.

They took credit for their wealth.

They thanked God for His blessings.

They believed their wealth proved God was pleased with them.

They became proud.

They generously gave to the needy.

They forgot God.

They sacrificially gave back to God.

2. What do you think? Does prosperity and comfort draw you closer to God? Or do you find yourself spending more time in prayer when you experience tough times?

3. How can we guard against the dangers of prosperity? Read these passages for guidance on how to stay close to the Lord even when we experience a time of blessing.

    a. Psalm 103:2

    b. Proverbs 30:8–9

    c. 1 Timothy 6:17–18

CREATE A PROJECT

1. We may not think of ourselves as wealthy, but in reality, the median individual income around the world is about $2,100 a year.[86] Most of us living in North America are rich compared to that. Let's take one step this week to guard against the dangers of prosperity. Based on the verses above, what is one thing you can do in the next seven days? Here are a few ideas:

   - Post Deuteronomy 8:11–18 where you can see it every day as a way to guard against forgetting God.

   - Remember the blessings God has given by keeping a gratitude journal. Every day this week, write down three or four things for which you are thankful.

   - Give to a charity that specifically helps people in poverty.

   - Help your children learn generosity by having them pick out some of their toys to give away.

   - Volunteer at a homeless shelter.

• My idea:

Here are some ideas if you're doing this study in a group:

- Do a Bible journaling project of Deuteronomy 8:11–18.

- Have participants write things they are grateful for on sticky notes and place them on a wall or poster board.

- Collect canned goods or socks to give to a local homeless shelter.

- Consider doing a service project together.

- Tell how this project changed you.

2. Praise God for His relentless love in song. Listen to "Your Love Never Fails" by Jesus Culture or "How He Loves" by David Crowder Band. Or sing a hymn like "My Song Is Love Unknown" (*LSB* 430) or "O the Deep, Deep Love of Jesus."[87]

CHAPTER EIGHT:
GOD'S RELENTLESS LOVE KNOWS NO BOUNDS

Study Questions

REFLECT ON THE READING

1. Heidi took her marriage vows seriously. She relentlessly loved Jim "for better or for worse." When have you witnessed that kind of love?

2. Name a favorite movie, book, or story that has a happily-ever-after conclusion. Why do you think we gravitate toward that kind of ending?

3. Circle the names you generally associate with God.

    Rule-Giver   Fun-Spoiler   Husband

    Lover   Stern-Judger   Confidant

    Why did you choose those?

4. What is your biggest takeaway from this chapter?

DIG INTO THE WORD

1. Read Hosea 14:2–3. Turn Hosea's example of a confession into your own personal words of repentance. (You don't have to share these with anyone.) Below, I have written a paraphrase of those verses to use as a guideline, if you wish.

> Take with you words
>
> and return to the Lord;
>
> say to Him,
>
> "Jesus, take away my sin of _____;
>
> accept my prayer of confession.
>
> I will pay with the sacrifice of my lips.
>
> I now realize that _____ can't save me;
>
> I can't get _____ through my own efforts.
>
> I'm done saying "My God"
>
> to _____.
>
> I know that in You, I—Your child—will find mercy."

2. Read Hosea 14:4–9.

    a. God spoke of a time when Israel would return as His beloved and described the blessings He would give in the future. Record some of the ways God would bless Israel.

b. Why do you think God used agricultural terms to describe His blessings?

c. God also used the image of a shadow. Read the following verses and write what you learn about living in God's shadow.
   Hosea 14:7

   Psalm 36:7

   Psalm 91:1

   Isaiah 51:16

d. After reading those passages, what does living in God's shadow mean to you?

Read Isaiah 62:4–5, 12:

You shall no more be termed Forsaken,
  and Your land shall no more be termed Desolate,
but you shall be called My Delight Is in Her,
  and your land Married;
for the LORD delights in you,
  and your land shall be married.
For as a young man marries a young woman,
  so shall your sons marry you,
and as the bridegroom rejoices over the bride,
  so shall your God rejoice over you. . . .
And they shall be called The Holy People,
  The Redeemed of the LORD;
and you shall be called Sought Out,
  A City Not Forsaken.

1. Before God's salvation, the people were called Desolate.

   a. What does *desolate* mean? (Look it up!)

b. When have you felt desolate?

2. Now circle all the positive names God gives His beloved. Which name means the most to you? Why?

CREATE A PROJECT

1. End your study with a wedding! Take this opportunity to picture yourself as God's beloved. Renew your vows to the God who relentlessly loves you.

Begin by setting the scene. Perhaps light some candles, and give everyone some flowers to hold. Play some soft classical music like "Canon in D" by Pachelbel or "Jesu, Joy of Man's Desiring" by J. S. Bach.

Next, listen to God's words of love for you. Read these promises of relentless love from the Book of Hosea. (If you are doing this with a group, have one person read them aloud, or take turns reading the statements.)

- Therefore, behold, I will allure her,
  and bring her into the wilderness,
  and speak tenderly to her. (Hosea 2:14)

- You must dwell as mine for many days. (Hosea 3:3)

- I desire steadfast love and not sacrifice,
  the knowledge of God rather than burnt offerings. (Hosea 6:6)

- Sow for yourselves righteousness;
  reap steadfast love;
  break up your fallow ground,

> for it is the time to seek the LORD,
>> that He may come and
>> rain righteousness upon you. (Hosea 10:12)

- I led them with cords of kindness, with the bands of love. (Hosea 11:4)

- My compassion grows warm and tender. (Hosea 11:8)

- I will love them freely. (Hosea 14:4)

- And in that day, declares the LORD, you will call Me "My Husband." . . . And I will betroth you to Me forever. I will betroth you to Me in righteousness and in justice, in steadfast love and in mercy. (Hosea 2:16, 19)

Take a moment to appreciate God's relentless love for you.

Then offer your own declaration of love and faithfulness. Write your own vows here:

Or, if you're doing this study with a group, say these words together as a reaffirmation God's loving calling to you:

I, _____, take You, Jesus, to be my lawfully wedded Savior from this day forward. In Your presence, and the presence of these witnesses, I promise to give You my faithfulness, my devotion, my all.

2. Close by singing a hymn like "Love Divine, All Loves Excelling" (*LSB* 700) or "O Perfect Love."[88] Other songs you might include are "Ever Be" by Aaron Shust and "Love Never Fails" by Brandon Heath.

CLOSING ACTIVITY

To review all you've learned in this study, fill out this simple chart. Look back in the study. Which Scriptures encouraged your heart? What did you learn that can help you live like you're loved by almighty God?

Chapter	Scripture That Encouraged Me	How I Can Live Like I'm Loved
1. God's Relentless Love Calls You His Own		
2. God's Relentless Love Pursues		
3. God's Relentless Love Redeems		
4. God's Relentless Love Restores		
5. God's Relentless Love Rains Righteousness		
6. God's Relentless Love Never Gives Up		
7. God's Relentless Love Disciplines		
8. God's Relentless Love Knows No Bounds		

PARTING THOUGHTS

We all long for love. Although we doubt anyone could love us just for who we are, our hearts desire that more than anything else. That's why I love the strange but beautiful story of Hosea. This book by an ancient prophet reassures us that God relentlessly loves us with an unwavering love—a love that is not based on our worth, achievement, or merit. It is a love based solely on Christ's work on the cross. We all have this love. Look at how God outlined this wonderful plan of salvation in His Word:

- "For all have sinned and fall short of the glory of God" (Romans 3:23). No one is perfect. Everyone fails to meet God's standard of sinlessness. This sin prevents us from coming to Him and from entering heaven.

- "For God so loved the world, that He gave His only Son, that whoever believes in Him should not perish but have eternal life" (John 3:16). God loved us so much that He sent His own Son to take the punishment we deserved for our sins and mistakes. Jesus' death enables us to live with God—forever.

- "For by grace you have been saved through faith. And this is not your own doing; it is the gift of God" (Ephesians 2:8). God gives us faith to believe in Jesus. His grace and mercy save us from death.

- "But to all who did receive Him, who believed in His name, He gave the right to become children of God" (John 1:12). By receiving Jesus in the waters of Baptism and the Holy Word of God, we become part of God's family.

I invite you to pray this prayer to the God who loves you and wants you to be part of His family:

Father in heaven, I realize that I am a sinner and fall short of what You want for my life. I know that I cannot save myself or earn eternal life. Thank You for sending Your Son, Jesus, to die for me. Through the power of His resurrection, You have made me alive eternally. Help me to turn from my sins and follow You. Thank You that although I may still fail, You will forgive me because Jesus paid the price for my sins. Thank You for Your gift of faith in Jesus, my Savior, and for the promise of eternal life with You. In Jesus' name I pray. Amen.

God speaks His words of relentless love and grace to you. Through God's free gift of faith in Jesus, you now are part of God's family!

ACKNOWLEDGMENTS

In many ways, this book has been the most difficult one to write. About halfway through, I seriously doubted my decision to tackle a Bible study on the Book of Hosea! I'm glad I persevered, because immersing myself in the relentless love of God for months has changed my heart and given me a new perspective.

But I could not have written this book alone. I wish to thank

God. Thank You for including the strange but beautiful story of Hosea and Gomer in Your Holy Word. Your persistent love for me has changed me forever. Resting in that love has enabled me to live in the freedom of Your embrace.

John. Thank you for your tenacious love for me over decades of marriage. For putting up with the hours I spend typing on the computer. For reading and rereading my words and offering excellent suggestions.

Family. To Mom, Anna and Nate, Nathaniel and Mary, Steven and Theresa, Shelly and David, Kathy and Bob—I thank you all for laughing and loving me through life.

Writing friends. Afton Rorvik, your encouragement kept me going when I felt like giving up on this project. Your wisdom and expertise made this a better book. Jan May, thank you for your friendship and support.

Those who lent their relentless love stories to the book. Thank you, Steven and Theresa, Shelly and David, Dick and Mary, Scott and Logan, Donna and Arlene, and Heidi. Your tales of unfailing devotion inspire us all.

Concordia Publishing House. Thanks to all who work so hard to edit, design, and market books that nurture faith in the God of relentless love. I owe a special thank-you to Peggy Kuethe, editor and friend, who makes writing for CPH a joy.

Answers

Chapter 1 Reflect on the Reading: Answers will vary. **Dig into the Word:** 1. a. Harsh Words (Law): Hosea 1:4–5: God will punish the house of Jehu, put an end to the kingdom of Israel, and break the bow of Israel in the valley of Jezreel. Hosea 1:6: God will not have mercy on Israel, will not forgive them. Hosea 1:9: God said Israel would no longer be His people; He would no longer be their God. Loving Words (Gospel): Hosea 1:11: The children of Israel and Judah will be gathered together and "great shall be the day of Jezreel." Hosea 2:1: Now God speaks: "You have received mercy." Hosea 1:10; 2:1: The nation would once again be called "Children of the living God" (1:10). God now says, "You are My people" (2:1). b. Words of Law: Romans 3:23: Everyone has sinned and fallen short of God's glory. Ephesians 2:1–2: We are dead in our trespasses and sins. Colossians 2:13a: We were dead in our sins and uncleanness. Words of Gospel: Romans 3:24–25: We are justified by the gift of God's grace through the redemption we have in Christ and which we receive by faith. Ephesians 2:8–9: By grace, we are saved through faith, not by works. Even faith is a gift. Colossians 2:13b–14: God made us alive, forgave our sins, and canceled our huge record of debt. c. Law shows our sin; exposes where we have failed. d. Law cannot make us right with God, but the Good News of the Gospel tells us that we can be made right with God through faith in Jesus Christ. e. Answers will vary. **Apply the Word to Your Life:** 1. a. Answers will vary but might include something like "I would have felt deep sorrow. Even if I no longer followed God faithfully, I still would have identified as belonging to God." b. Answers will vary. 2. a. Romans 9:26 quotes Hosea 1:10 almost word for word. b. It applies not only to the Jews but also to the Gentiles. c. Readers fill in their names. d. Answers will vary but might include a sense of belonging, love, support, care, and protection. e. God loves and cares for each of us. He promises His support when we feel weak and His protection when life gets scary. He tells us we belong to Him. f. Answers will vary. **Create a Project:** 1. a. Isaiah 43:1: Belonging to God; Romans 8:17: Heir; Romans 8:37: More Than Conqueror; 1 Peter 2:9: Chosen; 1 John 3:1: Child of God. b. Answers will vary. c. Answers will vary. d. Name tags. 2. Music.

Chapter 2 Reflect on the Reading: 1. Answers will vary. 2. God first takes Israel to court, accusing her of the crime of adultery. But His ultimate purpose is to court Israel—to woo her and bring her back to Him. 3. Answers will vary. 4. Answers will vary. **Dig into the Word:** 1. c. God constantly woos and pursues me, even when I have forgotten Him. God uses wilderness times to draw me closer to Him. d. God desires an intimate relationship with me. e. God will love me forever. f. God wants me to truly know Him. 2. Answers will vary. **Apply the Word to Your Life:** Answers will vary. **Create a Project:** Answers will vary.

Chapter 3 Reflect on the Reading: Answers will vary.

Dig into the Word:

Verse from Hosea	Related Verse	Theme of the Verses (Law)	Truth for Today (Gospel)
Hosea 3:1	Romans 5:8	Gomer didn't deserve Hosea's love. We don't deserve God's love.	Our feelings of shame and guilt can keep us from receiving God's love. The good news is that we can all have God's love because of His grace. We don't have to work for it or pretty ourselves up in order to deserve it.
Hosea 3:2	Titus 2:11–14	Hosea needed to redeem Gomer. Jesus gave Himself to redeem us.	Jesus paid the highest price possible to redeem us. That is how much we mean to Him!

Hosea 3:3	Isaiah 43:1	We belong to God. He calls us His own.	We all yearn to belong to someone who loves and cares for us. Even if we don't have that in an earthly relationship, we can all have the sense of belonging in Christ.
Hosea 3:4	Deuteronomy 6:13–14	Do not go after other gods.	Every culture has false gods. We must guard our hearts and avoid those gods.
Hosea 3:5	Jeremiah 29:13	Seek the Lord.	God longs for us to seek Him. He promises that if we seek Him, we will find Him.

Apply the Word to Your Life: 1. Answers will vary. 2. Answers will vary. 3. Answers will vary. 4. a. No, we are not saved because of our works, but because of God's purpose and grace. b. We are saved through faith in Christ Jesus, who abolished death and brought us life. 5. Answers will vary. **Create a Project:** 1. a. Ephesians 5:25–27: Paul uses the marriage relationship to describe how Christ loved the Church. 2 Corinthians 11:2: Paul says he betrothed the Corinthians to one husband, to Christ. Isaiah 54:5: The Creator of the world is our Husband and our Redeemer. Isaiah 62:5: God rejoices over us as a bridegroom rejoices over his bride. b. Create a collage. 2. Music.

Chapter 4 Reflect on the Reading: 1. Answers will vary. 2. Answers will vary but might include the following: Like a loving parent, God will do anything necessary to save His children, even sacrifice His only-begotten Son. Unlike an earthly parent, God is perfect and never makes a parenting mistake. 3. Answers will vary. Please remember that although we should not forget to go to almighty God for help, we can also use the services of doctors and counselors. God often uses these important people as means of healing. 4. Answers will vary. **Dig into the Word:** 1. Answers will vary; the table below contains examples of possible responses.

Chapter	Key Idea	God's Lesson for Israel	A Lesson for My Life
Hosea 4	God charges the people with a lack of faithfulness, love, and knowledge of God. He has special accusations and punishments for the priests.	God will punish Israel's unfaithfulness.	When I forget God, my life can fall apart (Hosea 4:6).
Hosea 5	God tells the priests, rulers, and people that they cannot hide their sin.	Don't rely on worldly sources of strength to save you.	God sometimes allows my human efforts to fail so that I will turn to Him (Hosea 5:13–15).
Hosea 6	Hosea calls out to the people to return to the God who can restore, but God sees their duplicitous hearts.	Return to God, who longs to restore you and bind up your wounds.	More than anything, God wants me to know Him personally and intimately (Hosea 6:6).

Hosea 7	God longs for Israel to repent and return to Him so that He can heal them, but they continue to turn to other nations for aid instead.	Return upward (Hosea 7:16). Cry out to God from your hearts.	When I have strayed away from God, He still longs for me to repent and return (Hosea 7:1, 16).

2. Answers will vary, but an example might include choosing the lesson "When I have strayed away from God, He still longs for me to repent and return" because sometimes I think God doesn't love me anymore when I've messed up. A specific action I could take would be to set aside time to pray and repent and then remind myself of God's promise of forgiveness (1 John 1:9). **Apply the Word to Your Life:** 1. Answers will vary. 2. Answers will vary. 3. Meanings of the word *know*: "to perceive, understand, to be aware, to be cognizant of." 4. Answers will vary. 5. Answers will vary but might include reading Christian books, meditating on God's Word, listening to sermons and Bible-based instruction, participating in the Lord's Supper. **Create a Project:** 1. Bandage project. 2. Music.

Chapter 5 Reflect on the Reading: Answers will vary. **Dig into the Word:** 1. Answers will vary. The table below contains examples of possible responses.

Chapter	Key Idea	God's Lesson for Israel	A Lesson for My Life
Hosea 8	God lists the sins of the Israelites: they have chosen their own kings, bowed down to idols, relied on foreign nations, and practiced cultic prostitution.	God sees their hypocrisy—they say they know God, but they don't really know Him (v. 2). They perform sacrifices but don't repent (v. 13).	Sometimes I make an idol out of silver and gold; I worship money (v. 4).
Hosea 9	God tells Israel, "The days of punishment have come" (v. 7).	Because the people have turned from Yahweh, He will allow Assyria to defeat them and carry them into exile.	Sometimes I forget about God and become more interested in my pet sins (v. 1).
Hosea 10	Yahweh disciplines His people so they will realize the foolishness of their false gods and seek Him again.	Even though God will punish Israel, His love for them never ends (vv. 11–12).	I rejoice that God's steadfast love never gives up on me (v. 12)!

2. Answers will vary. **Apply the Word to Your Life:** Answers will vary. **Create a Project:** Answers will vary.

Chapter 6 Reflect on the Reading: 1. Answers will vary. 2. Because God is love, He wanted to share that love and be loved in return. 3. Answers will vary. 4. Answers will vary. **Dig into the Word:** 1. Hosea 11 says the more God called out to Israel, the more they went away (v. 2). It talks about their worship and sacrifices to false gods (v. 2). They don't even recognize that God is the one who heals them (v. 3). The people are "bent" on turning away from God—their natural inclination is to run away from the One who loves them (v. 7). They call out to God, but God sees their hypocrisy (v. 7). 2. Hosea talks about God's love in terms of a father gently teaching his child how to walk (vv. 1, 3). God says that He simply cannot give up His people; His heart shudders at the thought (v. 8). We can see God's anger against His rebellious people, but also His decision not to execute it (v. 9). 3. God describes Himself as a loving Father (v. 1) who has a heart (v. 8). We witness His emotions—sadness when His beloved children don't respond to His love (v. 2), nostalgia when remembering when the relationship was good (vv. 3–4), anger over their unfaithfulness (v. 9). But unlike a man who would explode in rage and give up on these wayward people, God chooses not to execute His righteous anger (v. 9). He cannot bring Himself to forget them (v. 8).
Apply the Word to Your Life: 1. *The Tender Love of a Father.* Psalm 103:13: God loves us like a compassionate father loves his children. Luke 15:11–32: God the Father loves us even when we have shunned a relationship with Him and have viewed Him only as someone who can fulfill our needs and wants. He constantly watches for our return and welcomes us with open arms. 1 John 3:1: God shows His love by calling us His own children. He does not merely save us but welcomes us into His family. *The Compassion of an Animal Caretaker.* Psalm 23: As our Shepherd, God lovingly gives us rest, restoration, guidance, and comfort. Matthew 11:28–30: Jesus sees our burdens. He eases our yoke by getting in the yoke with us. He says His yoke is easy and His burden is light. John 10:7–15: Jesus describes Himself as the Good Shepherd who lays down His life for the sheep. In love, He will not abandon us. He has come to give us an abundant life. *The Mercy of a Judge.* Micah 7:18–19: God shows His love by pardoning our sin. In love, He delights to show mercy. In compassion, He hurls all our iniquities into the sea. John 5:21–

27: God the Father has given Jesus the authority to judge. And Jesus tells us that He will show mercy to all who believe His Word. Believers will not receive the death sentence they deserve. Instead, they will have life in heaven forever. Romans 8:1–2: We deserve condemnation, but because of the loving work of Jesus Christ, we have been set free. *The Roar of a Lion.* Hosea 5:14: Sometimes God's love disciplines His people so that they will seek Him once again. Joel 3:16: This verse speaks about Judgment Day. God will roar His judgment against the world, but He will be a refuge for His people. He will surround believers like a stronghold. God shows His love by protecting His children.[89] Revelation 5:5–6: Jesus is called the Lion of Judah from the root of David because He descended from the tribe of Judah and from King David's line. But the Lion became the Lamb who is slain—sacrificing Himself to atone for our sins. Jesus demonstrates His love in His willingness to give up His power and die for us. 2. Answers will vary. **Create a Project:** 1. Bracelet project. 2. Music.

Chapter 7 Reflect on the Reading: 1. Answers will vary. 2. We often discipline our children because we love them and we want what is best for them. We discipline them to teach them what is right and to protect them from danger. 3. Discipline does not always mean punishment. The Bible describes Job as "blameless and upright" (Job 1:1), yet he lost his wealth, his children, and his health. Joseph loyally served his Egyptian master, Potiphar, and even though he turned down Potiphar's wife's advances, he ended up in prison. The prophet Jeremiah faithfully spoke God's message to the Israelites, but he received only ridicule and mistreatment. The apostle Paul, after his conversion, worked tirelessly to spread the Gospel, but still he was flogged and imprisoned. 4. Answers will vary. **Dig into the Word:** 1. b. Hosea 13:3: The nation would disappear like mist, dew, chaff, or smoke. c. Hosea 13:7–8: Yahweh would destroy like a lion, leopard, or mother bear robbed of her cubs. d. Hosea 13:15: Agricultural disaster would come. Springs would dry up. The east wind also symbolizes Israel's enemy, Assyria, which would come and take the nation's treasury and wealth. e. Hosea 13:16: The capital city of Samaria would be destroyed by war. Women and children would be mutilated and slaughtered. 2. a. Hosea 12:6: God still invites Israel to return to Him; He will even help them repent and come back to Him. b. Hosea 13:4–5: Yahweh reminds them that He is the only God and Savior that they know. He knew them in the wilderness. c. Hosea 13:14: God has power over death and the grave. Although His compassion is hidden right now, someday, He will ransom and redeem those who trust in Him. **Apply the Word to Your Life:** 1. They took credit for their wealth. They believed their wealth proved God was pleased with them. They became proud. They forgot God. 2. Answers will vary. 3. a. Psalm 103:2: Remember the blessings God has given. Give Him the credit. b. Proverbs 30:8–9: Pray for neither poverty nor riches. Recognize that wealth can lead us to deny God. c. 1 Timothy 6:17–18: Realize the uncertainty and transience of riches. Be generous and share what God has given. **Create a Project:** 1. Individual or group project. 2. Music.

Chapter 8 Reflect on the Reading: Answers will vary. **Dig into the Word:** 1. Personalized prayer. 2. a. God will refresh them like dew refreshes the land. They will blossom like the lily. They will take root and the shoots will spread out. Their beauty will be like the olive and their fragrance like Lebanon. They will flourish like grain and blossom like a vine. b. Perhaps God used agricultural terms because the people were very familiar with the cycles of planting and harvest. They probably experienced both abundance and drought. Also, the people worshiped Baal and Asherah because they thought these gods would make their land fruitful. God wanted them to know He was in charge of nature. c. Hosea 14:7: When the people of Israel return, God will draw them so close that they will live in His shadow, where they will flourish. Psalm 36:7: The children of God take refuge in the shadow of His wings. Psalm 91:1: Dwelling in God's shadow provides shelter. Isaiah 51:16: The people of God live in the shadow of His hand. d. Answers will vary. **Apply the Word to Your Life:** 1. a. Barren, devastated; deserted, uninhabited; solitary, lonely; having the feeling of being abandoned by friends or by hope.[90] b. Answers will vary. 2. Answers will vary. **Create a Project:** 1. Wedding. 2. Music.

Closing Activity: Answers will vary.

ENDNOTES

1. Edward A. Engelbrecht, ed., *The Lutheran Study Bible* (St. Louis, MO: Concordia Publishing House, 2009), 603.
2. Paul E. Eickmann, *People's Bible Commentary: Hosea, Joel, Amos* (St. Louis, MO: Concordia Publishing House, 2005), 11.
3. https://www.blueletterbible.org/lang/lexicon/lexicon.cfm?strongs=H3808&t=KJV, accessed July 18, 2019.
4. https://www.blueletterbible.org/lang/lexicon/lexicon.cfm?strongs=H7355&t=KJV, accessed July 18, 2019.
5. https://www.blueletterbible.org/lang/lexicon/lexicon.cfm?strongs=H5971&t=KJV, accessed July 19, 2019.
6. https://www.blueletterbible.org/lang/lexicon/lexicon.cfm?Strongs=H5927&t=KJV, accessed July 19, 2019.
7. Eickmann, *People's Bible Commentary*, 19.
8. Edward A. Engelbrecht, ed., *Lutheran Bible Companion, Vol. 1: Introduction and Old Testament* (St. Louis, MO: Concordia Publishing House, 2014), 861.
9. *The Lutheran Study Bible*, 1927–28.
10. Douglas Stuart, *Word Biblical Commentary, Vol. 31: Hosea–Jonah* (Nashville, TN: Word, Incorporated, 1987), 54. Used by permission of Thomas Nelson. www.thomasnelson.com
11. Stuart, *Word Biblical Commentary*, 54.
12. Eickmann, *People's Bible Commentary*, 5.
13. Stuart, *Word Biblical Commentary*, 49.
14. Eickmann, *People's Bible Commentary*, 23.
15. https://www.blueletterbible.org/lang/lexicon/lexicon.cfm?Strongs=H1540&t=KJV, accessed August 14, 2019.
16. Stuart, *Word Biblical Commentary*, 53.
17. Eickmann, *People's Bible Commentary*, 28.
18. Eickmann, *People's Bible Commentary*, 31.
19. *The Lutheran Study Bible*, 1431.
20. Henri J. M. Nouwen, *You Are the Beloved: Daily Meditations for Spiritual Living* (New York: Convergent Books, 2017), 76, Kindle.
21. Geoffrey R. Boyle, *LifeLight Leaders Guide: Hosea/Joel/Amos* (St. Louis, MO: Concordia Publishing House, 2014), 17.
22. Some scholars, in looking at Middle Assyrian laws of the day, propose that Hosea needed to extricate her from a legal problem she couldn't free herself from—such as a debt she owed. *NKJV Cultural Backgrounds Study Bible: Bringing to Life the Ancient World of Scripture* (Grand Rapids, MI: Zondervan, 2017), loc. 163743 of 301470, Kindle.
23. Robert Alter, *The Art of Biblical Narrative* (New York: Basic Books [A Member of the Perseus Books Group], 1983), 93.
24. *Luther's Small Catechism with Explanation* (St. Louis, MO: Concordia Publishing House, 2017), 100.
25. Eickmann, *People's Bible Commentary*, 63.
26. Stuart, *Word Biblical Commentary*, 119.
27. Eickmann, *People's Bible Commentary*, 65.
28. Stuart, *Word Biblical Commentary*, 121.
29. Stuart, *Word Biblical Commentary*, 101.
30. *The Lutheran Study Bible*, 529.
31. Robert G. Hoerber, ed., *Concordia Self-Study Bible: New International Version* (St. Louis, MO: Concordia Publishing House, 1986), 552.
32. *NIV Archaeological Study Bible: An Illustrated Walk Through Biblical History and Culture* (Grand Rapids, MI: Zondervan, 2005), 556.
33. *Concordia Self-Study Bible*, 551.
34. *Concordia Self-Study Bible*, 550.
35. Eickmann, *People's Bible Commentary*, 56.
36. W. E. Vine, Merrill F. Unger, William White Jr., *Vine's Complete Expository Dictionary of Old and New Testament Words* (Nashville, TN: Thomas Nelson, 1985), Old Testament Section, 130.
37. Boyle, *LifeLight Leaders Guide*, 20.
38. Stuart, *Word Biblical Commentary*, 154.
39. *The Lutheran Study Bible*, 1440.
40. Eickmann, *People's Bible Commentary*, 93.
41. *The Lutheran Study Bible*, 1439.
42. Stuart, *Word Biblical Commentary*, 153.
43. *The Lutheran Study Bible*, 1769.
44. *Concordia: The Lutheran Confessions*, 2nd ed. (St. Louis: Concordia Publishing House, 2006), 359.
45. *The Lutheran Study Bible*, 1438.
46. *Concordia: The Lutheran Confessions*, 361.
47. *NIV Archaeological Study Bible*, 504.
48. *NKJV Cultural Backgrounds Study Bible*, loc. 163871 of 301470, Kindle.
49. *The Lutheran Study Bible*, 1434.
50. Eickmann, *People's Bible Commentary*, 88.
51. Eickmann, *People's Bible Commentary*, 96.
52. https://www.blueletterbible.org/lang/lexicon/lexicon.cfm?Strongs=H2015&t=KJV, accessed December 9, 2019.
53. Stuart, *Word Biblical Commentary*, 182.
54. Stuart, *Word Biblical Commentary*, 184.
55. Rudolph F. Norden, *Hosea: Critic and Comforter for Today* (St. Louis, MO: Concordia Publishing House, 1996), 105.

56. *The Lutheran Study Bible*, 1442.
57. Stuart, *Word Biblical Commentary*, 183.
58. *The Lutheran Study Bible*, 1442.
59. Eickmann, *People's Bible Commentary*, 101.
60. *The Lutheran Study Bible*, 53.
61. *The Lutheran Study Bible*, 67.
62. *The Lutheran Study Bible*, 67.
63. *NKJV Cultural Backgrounds Study Bible*, loc. 163942 of 301470, Kindle.
64. *NKJV Cultural Backgrounds Study Bible*, loc. 104404 of 301470, Kindle.
65. *The Lutheran Study Bible*, 1443.
66. *The Lutheran Study Bible*, 128.
67. Stuart, *Word Biblical Commentary*, 209.
68. Eickmann, *People's Bible Commentary*, 108.
69. *The Lutheran Study Bible*, 1444.
70. Eickmann, *People's Bible Commentary*, 111.
71. Paul E. Kretzmann, *Popular Commentary of the Bible: The Old Testament, Volume II* (St. Louis, MO: Concordia Publishing House, 1924), 649.
72. Kretzmann, *Popular Commentary of the Bible*, 650.
73. *NIV Archaeological Study Bible*, 1430.
74. Eickmann, *People's Bible Commentary*, 114.
75. *The Lutheran Study Bible*, 1443.
76. https://www.blueletterbible.org/lang/lexicon/lexicon.cfm?Strongs=H6960&t=KJV, accessed January 9, 2020.
77. *The Lutheran Study Bible*, 1446.
78. *Luther's Small Catechism with Explanation*, 205.
79. Eickmann, *People's Bible Commentary*, 121–22.
80. Sharla Fritz, *Waiting: A Bible Study on Patience, Hope, and Trust* (St. Louis, MO: Concordia Publishing House, 2017), 130.
81. https://hymnary.org/media/fetch/116976, accessed March 13, 2020.
82. Boyle, *LifeLight Leaders Guide*, 18.
83. Boyle, *LifeLight Leaders Guide*, 17.
84. *Concordia: The Lutheran Confessions*, 359.
85. Adapted from https://happyhourprojects.com/quick-and-easy-leather-wrap-bracelet/, accessed December 12, 2019.
86. https://www.washingtonpost.com/news/monkey-cage/wp/2018/08/23/most-americans-vastly-underestimate-how-rich-they-are-compared-with-the-rest-of-the-world-does-it-matter/, accessed January 11, 2020.
87. https://hymnary.org/media/fetch/97624, accessed March 13, 2020.
88. https://hymnary.org/media/fetch/139498, accessed March 13, 2020.
89. Eickmann, *People's Bible Commentary*, 172.
90. https://www.dictionary.com/browse/desolate?s=t, accessed January 28, 2020.

NOTES

NOTES

NOTES